The Philosophical Baby

*What Children's Minds Tell Us about Truth,
Love & the Meaning of Life*

The Philosophical Baby

*What Children's Minds Tell Us about Truth,
Love & the Meaning of Life*

ALISON GOPNIK

THE BODLEY HEAD
LONDON

Published by The Bodley Head 2009

2 4 6 8 10 9 7 5 3 1

Copyright © Alison Gopnik 2009

Alison Gopnik has asserted her right under the Copyright, Designs
and Patents Act 1988 to be identified as the author of this work

First published in Great Britain in 2009 by
The Bodley Head
Random House, 20 Vauxhall Bridge Road,
London SW1V 2SA

www.bodleyhead.co.uk
www.rbooks.co.uk

Addresses for companies within The Random House Group Limited can be found at:
www.randomhouse.co.uk/offices.htm

The Random House Group Limited Reg. No. 954009

A CIP catalogue record for this book
is available from the British Library

ISBN 9781847921079 (TPB)

The Random House Group Limited supports The Forest Stewardship
Council (FSC), the leading international forest certification organisation. All our titles
that are printed on Greenpeace approved FSC certified paper carry the FSC logo.
Our paper procurement policy can be found at
www.rbooks.co.uk/environment

Mixed Sources
Product group from well-managed
forests and other controlled sources
www.fsc.org Cert no. TT-COC-2139
© 1996 Forest Stewardship Council
FSC

Printed and bound in Great Britain by
Clays Ltd, St Ives PLC

TO BLAKE, MY PHILOSOPHICAL BABY BROTHER,

WITH PROFOUND GRATITUDE FOR THE TRUTH AND LOVE

HE HAS ALWAYS GIVEN ME

Contents

✳

2. Imaginary Companions:
How Does Fiction Tell the Truth?   47

3. Escaping Plato's Cave: How Children, Scientists,
and Computers Discover the Truth   74

4. What Is It Like to Be a Baby?
Consciousness and Attention   106

5. Who Am I? Memory, Self, and the Babbling Stream   133

6. Heraclitus' River and the Romanian Orphans: How Does Our Early Life Shape Our Later Life?   164

7. Learning to Love: Attachment and Identity   179

8. Love and Law: The Origins of Morality   202

9. Babies and the Meaning of Life   234

The Philosophical Baby

Introduction

＊

A one-month-old stares at her mother's face with fixed, brow-wrinkling concentration, and suddenly produces a beatific smile. Surely she must see her mother and feel love, but what are seeing and feeling like for her? What is it like to be a baby? A two-year-old offers a hungry-looking stranger a half-chewed lollipop. Could a child this young already feel empathy and be altruistic? A three-year-old announces that she will come to dinner only if a place is laid for the Babies, the tiny purple-haired twins who live in her pocket and eat flowers for breakfast. How could she believe so profoundly in something that is just a figment of her own imagination? And how could she dream up such remarkable creatures? A five-year-old discovers, with the help of a goldfish, that death is irreversible. How could a child who can't yet read or add uncover deep, hard truths about mortality? The one-month-old turns into the two-year-old and then the three-year-old and the five-year-old and eventually, miraculously, turns into a mother with children of her own. How could all these utterly different creatures be the same person? All of us once were children and most of us will become parents—we have all asked these sorts of questions.

Childhood is a profound part of the human condition. But it is also a largely unexamined part of that condition—so taken for granted that most of the time we hardly notice it at all. Childhood is a universal fact, but when we do think about it, it is almost always in individual first-person terms: What should I do, now, about *my* child? What did *my* parents do that led *me* to be the way I am? Most books about children are like this, from memoirs and novels to the ubiquitous parenting advice books. But childhood is not just a particular plot complication of Irish autobiographies or a particular problem to be solved by American self-help programs. It is not even just something that all human beings share. It is, I'll argue, what makes all human beings human.

When we start to think about childhood more deeply, we realize that this universal, apparently simple fact is riddled with complexities and contradictions. Children are, at once, deeply familiar and profoundly alien. Sometimes we feel that they are just like us—and sometimes they seem to live in a completely different world. Their minds seem drastically limited; they know so much less than we do. And yet long before they can read or write they have extraordinary powers of imagination and creativity, and long before they go to school they have remarkable learning abilities. Their experience of the world sometimes seems narrow and concrete; at other times it looks far more wide-ranging than adult experience. It seems that our experiences as children were crucial in shaping who we are. And yet we all know that the path from child to adult is circuitous and complex, and that the world is full of saints with terrible parents and neurotics with loving ones.

The younger children are, the more mysterious they are. We can more or less remember what it was like to be five or six, and we can talk with school-age children on a reasonably equal basis. But babies and toddlers are utterly foreign territory. Babies can't walk or talk, and even toddlers, well, toddle, and yet science, and indeed common sense, tells us that in those early years they are learning more than they ever will again. It may be hard to see just how the child is father to the man. Yet it is even more difficult to trace the link between the "I" writing this page and the seven-pound bundle of fifty years ago, all eyes and forehead, or even the later thirty-pound whirlwind of tangled sentences, intense emotions, and wild pretend play. We don't even have a good name for this age range. This book will focus on children under five and I'll sometimes use the word "babies" to talk about anybody younger than three. For me "babies" means that particularly adorable combination of chubby cheeks and funny pronunciation, though I recognize that many three-year-olds themselves would reject the description vigorously.

New scientific research and philosophical thinking have both illuminated and deepened the mystery. In the last thirty years, there's been a revolution in our scientific understanding of babies and young children. We used to think that babies and young children were irrational, egocentric, and amoral. Their thinking and experience were concrete, immediate, and limited. In fact, psychologists and neuroscientists have discovered that babies not only learn more, but imagine more, care more, and experience more than we would ever have thought possible. In some ways, young children are actually smarter, more imaginative, more caring, and even more conscious than adults are.

This scientific revolution has led philosophers to take babies seriously for the first time. Children are both profound and puzzling, and this combination is the classic territory of philosophy. Yet you could read 2,500 years of philosophy and find almost nothing about children. A Martian who tried to figure us out by studying Earthling philosophy could easily conclude that human beings reproduce by asexual cloning. The index of the thousands of pages in the 1967 *Encyclopedia of Philosophy* had no references to babies, infants, families, parents, mothers, or fathers, and only four to children at all. (There are hundreds of references to angels and the morning star.)

Very recently, however, this has begun to change. Philosophers have started to pay attention to babies and even to learn from them. The current *Encyclopedia of Philosophy* includes articles that are actually about babies, with titles such as "Infant Cognition" and "The Child's Theory of Mind." I talk at the American Philosophical Association as well as the Society for Research in Child Development, and philosophers argue about when babies understand the minds of others, how they learn about the world, and whether they are capable of empathy. A few even sit precariously on little chairs in preschools and do experiments with children. Thinking about babies and young children can help answer fundamental questions about imagination, truth, consciousness, identity, love, and morality in a new way. In this book I'll argue for a new view of these fundamental philosophical ideas, based on babies, and a new view of babies, based on these philosophical ideas.

HOW CHILDREN CHANGE THE WORLD

There's one big, general idea behind all the specific experiments and arguments in this book. More than any other creature, human beings are able to change. We change the world around us, other people, and ourselves. Children, and childhood, help explain how we change. And the fact that we change explains why children are the way they are—and even why childhood exists at all.

Ultimately, the new scientific explanations of childhood are rooted in evolutionary theory. But studying children leads to a very different picture of how evolution shapes our lives than the traditional picture of "evolutionary psychology." Some psychologists and philosophers argue that most of what is significant about human nature is determined by our genes—an innate hardwired system that makes us who we are. We're endowed with a set of fixed and distinct abilities, designed to suit the needs of our prehistoric ancestors 200,000 years ago in the Pleistocene. Not surprisingly, this view discounts the importance of childhood. The picture is that a "good enough" childhood environment may be necessary to let the innate aspects of human nature unfold. But beyond that, childhood won't have much influence because most of what is important about human nature in general, and individual character in particular, is in place at birth.

But this view doesn't capture our lives as we actually live them and as they change and develop over time. We at least feel as if we actively create our lives, changing our world and our selves. This view also can't explain the radical historical changes in human life. If our nature is determined by our genes, you would think that we would be the same now as we were in the Pleistocene. The puzzling fact about human beings is that our capacity for change, both in our own lives and through history, is the most distinctive and unchanging thing about us. Is there a way of explaining this flexibility and creativity, this ability to alter our individual and collective fate, without resorting to mysticism?

The answer, unexpectedly, comes from very young children—and it leads to a very different kind of evolutionary psychology. The great evolutionary advantage of human beings is their ability to escape from the constraints of evolution. We can learn about our environment, we can imagine different environments, and we can turn those imagined environments into reality. And as an intensely social species, other people are the most important part of our environment. So we are particularly likely to learn about people and to use that knowledge to change the way other people behave, and the way we behave ourselves. The result is that human beings, as a central part of their evolutionary endowment, and as the deepest part of their human nature, are engaged in a constant cycle of change. We change our surroundings and our surroundings change us. We alter other people's behavior, their behavior alters ours.

We begin with the capacity to learn more effectively and more flexibly about our environment than any other species. This knowledge lets us imagine new environments, even radically new environments, and act to change the existing ones. Then we can learn about the unexpected features of the new environment that we have created, and so change that environment once again and so on. What neuroscientists call plasticity—the ability to change in the light of experience—is the key to human nature at every level from brains to minds to societies.

Learning is a key part of the process, but the human capacity for change goes beyond just learning. Learning is about the way the world changes our mind, but our minds can also change the world. Developing a new theory about the world allows us to imagine other ways the world might be. Understanding other people and ourselves lets us imagine new ways of being human. At the same time, to change our world, our selves, and our society we have to think about what we ought to be like, as well as what we actually are like. This book is about how children develop minds that change the world.

Psychologists, philosophers, neuroscientists, and computer

scientists are beginning to carefully and precisely identify some of the underlying mechanisms that give us this distinctively human capacity for change—the aspects of our nature that allow nurture and culture to take place. We even are starting to develop rigorous mathematical accounts of some of those mechanisms. We'll see that this new research and thinking, much of it done just in the past few years, has given us a new understanding of how the biological computers in our skulls actually produce human freedom and flexibility.

If I look around at the ordinary things in front of me as I write this—the electric lamp, the right-angle-constructed table, the brightly glazed symmetrical ceramic cup, the glowing computer screen—almost nothing resembles anything I would have seen in the Pleistocene. All of these objects were once imaginary—they are things that human beings themselves have created. And I myself, a woman cognitive scientist writing about the philosophy of children, could not have existed in the Pleistocene either. I am also a creation of the human imagination, and so are you.

HOW CHILDHOOD CHANGES THE WORLD

The very fact of childhood—our long protected period of immaturity—plays a crucial role in this human ability to change the world and ourselves. Children aren't just defective adults, primitive grown-ups gradually attaining our perfection and complexity. Instead, children and adults are different forms of *Homo sapiens*. They have very different, though equally complex and powerful, minds, brains, and forms of consciousness, designed to serve different evolutionary functions. Human development is more like metamorphosis, like caterpillars becoming butterflies, than like simple growth—though it may seem that children are the vibrant, wandering butterflies who transform into caterpillars inching along the grown-up path.

What *is* childhood? It's a distinctive developmental period in which young human beings are uniquely dependent on adults. Childhood literally couldn't exist without caregivers. Why do we go through a period of childhood at all? Human beings have a much more extended period of immaturity and dependence, a much longer childhood, than other species, and this period of immaturity has become longer as human history has gone on (as we parents of twenty-somethings may recognize with a sigh). Why make babies so helpless for so long, and why make adults invest so much time and energy in caring for them?

This protracted period of immaturity is intimately tied up with the human capacity for change. Our human capacities for imagination and learning have great advantages; they allow us to adapt to more different environments than any other species and to change our own environments in a way that no other animal can. But they also have one great disadvantage—learning takes time. You don't want to be stuck exploring all the new possible ways to hunt deer when you haven't eaten for two days, or learning all the accumulated cultural wisdom about saber-toothed tigers when one is chasing you. It would be a good idea for me to spend a week exploring all the capabilities of my new computer, as my teenage son would, but with the saber-toothed tigers of grant deadlines and classes breathing down my neck, I'll just go on relying on the old routines.

An animal that depends on the accumulated knowledge of past generations has to have some time to acquire that knowledge. An animal that depends on imagination has to have some time to exercise it. Childhood is that time. Children are protected from the usual exigencies of adult life; they don't need to hunt deer or ward off saber-toothed tigers, let alone write grant proposals or teach classes—all of that is done for them. All they need to do is learn. When we're children we're devoted to learning about our world and imagining all the other ways that world could be. When we become adults we put all that we've learned and imagined to use.

There's a kind of evolutionary division of labor between children and adults. Children are the R&D department of the human species—the blue-sky guys, the brainstormers. Adults are production and marketing. They make the discoveries, we implement them. They think up a million new ideas, mostly useless, and we take the three or four good ones and make them real.

If we focus on adult abilities, long-term planning, swift and automatic execution, rapid skillful reaction to the deer and the tigers and the deadlines, then babies and young children will indeed look pretty pathetic. But if we focus on our distinctive capacities for change, especially imagination and learning, then it's the adults who look slow. The caterpillars and butterflies do different things well.

This basic division of labor between children and adults is reflected in their minds, their brains, their everyday activities, and even their conscious experience. Babies' brains seem to have special qualities that make them especially well suited for imagination and learning. Babies' brains are actually more highly connected than adult brains; more neural pathways are available to babies than adults. As we grow older and experience more, our brains "prune out" the weaker, less used pathways and strengthen the ones that are used more often. If you looked at a map of the baby's brain it would look like old Paris, with lots of winding, interconnected little streets. In the adult brain those little streets have been replaced by fewer but more efficient neural boulevards, capable of much more traffic. Young brains are also much more plastic and flexible—they change much more easily. But they are much less efficient; they don't work as quickly or effectively.

There are even more specific brain changes that play a particularly important role in the metamorphosis from childhood to adulthood. They involve the prefrontal cortex, a part of the brain that is uniquely well developed in human beings, and that neuroscientists often argue is the seat of distinctively human abilities. Scientists have located sophisticated capacities for thinking, planning, and control in the prefrontal area. For example, through a tragic combination of error and arrogance, psychiatric patients in the fifties were subjected to prefrontal lobotomies—operations that removed this part of their brains. Although these patients remained superficially functional, they had largely lost the ability to make decisions, to control their impulses, and to act intelligently.

The prefrontal cortex is one of the last parts of the brain to mature. The wiring of this part of the cortex, the process of pruning out some connections and strengthening others, may not be complete until the mid-twenties (another sigh from parents of twenty-somethings). Recently neuroscientists have discovered that all of the brain is more plastic and changeable, even in adulthood, than we ever thought before. Still, some parts, the visual system, for example, seem to take their adult form in the first few months of life. Others, like the prefrontal cortex, and the connections between the prefrontal area and other parts of the brain, mature much more slowly. They continue to change through adolescence and beyond. The visual cortex is much the same at six months and sixty, while the prefrontal area takes on its final form only in adulthood.

You might think this means that children are defective adults, that they lack the parts of the brain that are most crucial for rational adult thought. But you could equally say that, when it comes to imagination and learning, prefrontal immaturity allows children to be superadults. The prefrontal cortex is especially involved in "inhibition." It actually helps shut down other parts of the brain, limiting and focusing experience, action, and thought. This process is crucial for the complex thinking, planning, and acting that adults engage in. To execute a complex plan, for example, you have to perform just the actions that are dictated by that plan, and not all the other possible actions. And you have to pay attention to just the events that are relevant to your plan and not all the others. Anyone who tries to persuade a three-year-old to get dressed for preschool will develop an appreciation of inhibition. It would be so much easier if he didn't stop to explore every speck of dust on the floor, pull out all the drawers in turn, and take off his socks just after you've put them on.

But, as we'll see, inhibition has a downside if you are primarily interested in imagination and learning. To be imaginative, you want to consider as many possibilities as you can, even wild and unprecedented ones (maybe the dresser would work better without all those drawers). In learning, you want to remain open to anything that may turn out to be the truth (maybe that speck of dust holds the secret of the universe). The lack of strong prefrontal control may actually be a benefit of childhood.

In another sense the prefrontal cortex is the *most* active part of the brain during childhood, it constantly changes throughout those years, and its final form depends heavily on childhood experience. The powers of imagination and learning during childhood provide us with the information that we adults use to plan and control our behavior intelligently. In fact, there is some evidence that high IQ is correlated with later maturing and more plastic frontal lobes. Keeping your mind open longer may be part of what makes you smarter.

Those different brains and minds mean that adults and children also spend their days differently—we work, babies play. Play is the signature of childhood. It's a living, visible manifestation of imagination and learning in action. It's also the most visible sign of the paradoxically useful uselessness of immaturity. By definition, play—the baby nesting blocks and pushing the buttons of a busy box, the toddler pretending to be everything from a mermaid to a ninja—has no obvious point or goal or function. It does nothing to advance the basic evolutionary goals of mating and predation, fleeing and fighting. And yet these useless actions—and the adult equivalents we squeeze into our workday—are distinctively, characteristically human and deeply valuable. Plays are play, and so are novels, paintings, and songs.

All these differences between children and adults suggest that children's consciousness, the texture of their everyday experience of the world, must be very different from ours. Children's brains and minds are radically different from ours, so their experience must be too. These differences are not just a source of idle wonder. We can actually use what we know about children's minds and brains to explore their consciousness. We can use the tools of psychology, neuroscience, and philosophy to understand the inner lives of children. In turn, understanding children's consciousness gives us a new perspective on our everyday adult consciousness and on what it means to be human.

These differences also raise intriguing questions about identity. Babies and adults are radically different creatures with different minds, brains, and experiences. But from another perspective we adults are just the final product of childhood. Our brains are the brains that were shaped by experience, our lives are the lives that began as babies, our consciousness is the consciousness that reaches back to childhood. The Greek philosopher Heraclitus said that no man ever steps in the same river twice because neither the river nor the man is the same. Thinking about children and childhood makes it vivid that our lives, and our history as a species, are that sort of ever-changing perpetually flowing river.

All the processes of change, imagination, and learning ultimately depend on love. Human caregivers love their babies in a particularly intense and significant way. That love is one of the engines of human change. Parental love isn't just a primitive and primordial instinct, continuous with the nurturing behavior of other animals (though certainly there are such continuities). Instead, our extended life as parents also plays a deep role in the emergence of the most sophisticated and characteristically human capacities. Our protracted immaturity is possible only because we can rely on the love of the people who take care of us. We can learn from the discoveries of earlier generations because those same loving caregivers invest in teaching us. It isn't just that without mothering humans would lack nurturance, warmth, and emotional security. They would also lack culture, history, morality, science, and literature.

A ROAD MAP

In the first three chapters of this book, I'll explore the philosophical thinking and psychological research behind our new understanding of imagination and learning. Even the youngest babies know a great deal about how the world works. And yet toddlers spend most of their waking hours in wild pretend worlds, politely drinking imaginary tea and ferociously battling imaginary tigers. Why? In chapter 1, I'll explain how knowledge and imagination are intertwined. Children use their knowledge to construct alternate universes—different ways the world might be.

Children also know a great deal about how people work. This lets them imagine new ways that people, including themselves, might think or act. In chapter 2, I'll explain how those abilities lead children to create imaginary friends—and lead grown-ups to create plays and novels. Imagining how they could be different actually lets children, and adults, become different. We can turn ourselves into our imaginary alter egos.

In chapter 3, I'll show where knowledge and imagination come from. Philosophers of science and computer scientists have developed new ideas about how learning and imagination are possible—ideas that have actually been used to design computers that can learn and imagine. These ideas can also explain how children learn and imagine as much as they do. I'll show that babies, like scientists, use statistics and experiments to learn about the world. But they also have a particularly powerful and distinctively human way of learning: they have caregivers who teach them. These kinds of learning allow us to constantly change our view of the world and of the possibilities it offers.

In the next two chapters I'll talk about consciousness. Is the way we see the world as adults the way we always have and always will see the world? Or could consciousness itself change? What is it like to be a baby? There are two very different aspects of consciousness in grown-ups. First there is our external consciousness—our vivid awareness of the world outside us, the blue of the sky, the song of the birds. In chapter 4, I'll describe new studies of babies' minds and brains, and especially babies' attention. Babies attend to the world in a very different way than we do, and this kind of attention is related to their extraordinary learning abilities. I'll argue that babies are actually more conscious than we are, more vividly aware of everything that goes on around them.

We also experience internal consciousness. This is the stream of thoughts, feelings, and plans that seem to run past that inner "I" who is also the inner "eye"—the internal observer, autobiographer, and executive we call our self. In chapter 5, I'll argue that this internal consciousness may be quite different for babies and toddlers, and adults. Babies experience the past and the future, memory and desire, very differently than we do. They don't seem to have the same kind of inner observer, and they remember the past and plan for the future in very different ways. A single unified self is something we create—not something we are given.

In the next three chapters, I'll consider what these new ideas can tell us about another set of questions—questions about identity, love, and morality. These are often the most urgent questions for us as parents of our children, and indeed as children of our parents. In chapter 6, I'll talk about the relation between our lives as children and our lives as adults. How do the experiences and actions of childhood shape our later experiences and actions? How does our childhood make us who we are? In chapter 7, I'll focus on a particular part of this question. Where does the love between parents and children come from? How does it shape our adult loves and lives? I'll argue that we aren't simply determined by either our genes or our mothers. Instead, our childhood experiences guide the way we create our own lives.

In chapter 8, I'll explain what children tell us about our moral lives. Babies and young children are not the amoral creatures we once thought. Even the youngest babies have striking capacities for empathy and altruism. And even toddlers know that rules should be followed but that they can be changed. These two capacities,

capacities for love and law, for caring about others and following the rules, allow our characteristically human combination of moral depth and flexibility. They explain how we can change our laws and rules to suit new circumstances without falling into moral relativism.

Finally, in chapter 9, I'll talk about the spiritual significance of babies—about babies and the meaning of life. For most parents, raising children is one of the most significant, meaningful, and profound experiences of their lives. Is this just an evolutionary illusion, a trick to make us keep on reproducing? I'll argue that it's the real thing, that children really do put us in touch with truth, beauty, and meaning.

Nothing in this book will help parents get their children to sleep or send them to a good college or guarantee them a happy adult life. But I hope it will help parents, and people who aren't parents too, to appreciate the richness and significance of childhood in a new way. Even the most mundane facts of three-year-old life—the extravagant pretend play, the insatiable curiosity that makes them get into just about everything, and the intuitive sympathy for others—tell us what it means to be human. Philosophy and science can help us understand how our children think and feel and experience the world—and how we do too.

I.

Possible Worlds

WHY DO CHILDREN PRETEND?

✳

Human beings don't live in the real world. The real world is what actually happened in the past, is happening now, and will happen in the future. But we don't just live in this single world. Instead, we live in a universe of many possible worlds, all the ways the world could be in the future and also all the ways the world could have been in the past, or might be in the present. These possible worlds are what we call dreams and plans, fictions and hypotheses. They are the products of hope and imagination. Philosophers, more drily, call them "counterfactuals."

Counterfactuals are the woulda-coulda-shouldas of life, all the things that might happen in the future, but haven't yet, or that could have happened in the past, but didn't quite. Human beings care deeply about those possible worlds—as deeply as they care about the real actual world. On the surface counterfactual thinking seems like a very sophisticated and philosophically puzzling ability. How can we think about things that aren't there? And why should we think this way instead of restricting ourselves to the actual world? It seems obvious that understanding the real world would give us an evolutionary edge, but what good do we get from imaginary worlds?

We can start to answer these questions by looking at young children. Is counterfactual thought present only in sophisticated grown-ups? Or can young children think about possibilities too? The conventional wisdom, echoed in the theories of both Sigmund Freud and Jean Piaget, is that babies and young children are limited to the here and now—their immediate sensations and perceptions and experience. Even when young children pretend or imagine they can't distinguish between reality and fantasy: their fantasies, in this view, are just another kind of immediate experience. Counterfactual thought requires a more demanding ability to understand the relation between reality and all the alternatives to that reality.

Cognitive scientists have discovered that this conventional picture is wrong. We've found out that even very young children can already consider possibilities, distinguish them from reality, and even use them to change the world. They can imagine different ways the world might be in the future and use them to create plans. They can imagine different ways the world might have been in the past, and reflect on past possibilities. And, most dramatically, they can create completely imaginary worlds, wild fictions, and striking pretenses. These crazy imaginary worlds are a familiar part of childhood—every parent of a three-year-old has exclaimed, "What an imagination!" But the new research profoundly changes the way we think about those worlds.

In the past ten years we've not only discovered that children have these imaginative powers—we've actually begun to understand how these powers are possible. We are developing a science of the imagination. How could children's minds and brains be constructed to allow them to imagine this dazzling array of alternate universes?

The answer is surprising. Conventional wisdom suggests that knowledge and imagination, science and fantasy, are deeply different from one another—even opposites. But the new ideas I'll outline show that exactly the same abilities that let children learn so much about the world also allow them to change the world—to bring new worlds into existence—and to imagine alternative worlds that may never exist at all. Children's brains create causal theories of the world, maps of how the world works. And these theories allow children to envisage new possibilities, and to imagine and pretend that the world is different.

THE POWER OF COUNTERFACTUALS

Psychologists have found that counterfactual thinking is absolutely pervasive in our everyday life and deeply affects our judgments, our decisions, and our emotions. You would think that what really matters is what actually happens, not what you imagine might have happened in the past or could happen in the future. This is particularly true of counterfactuals about the past—what might have happened but didn't—the woulda-coulda-shouldas of life. Yet the woulda-coulda-shouldas have a deep impact on experience.

In one experiment, the Nobel Prize–winning psychologist Daniel Kahneman and his colleagues asked people to imagine the following sort of scenario. Mr. Tees and Mr. Crane are both in a taxi to the airport, desperate to catch their respective planes, which are both scheduled to take off at 6:00. But traffic is impossibly snarled and the minutes tick by. Finally, at 6:30 they arrive at the airport. It turns out that Mr. Tees's flight left at 6:00 as planned but Mr. Crane's flight was delayed till 6:25 and Mr. Crane sees it take off as he arrives. Who is more upset?

Just about everyone agrees that Mr. Crane, who just missed his flight, will be much more unhappy. But why? They both missed their flights. It seems that what is making Mr. Crane unhappy is not the actual world but the counterfactual worlds, the ones in which the taxi arrived just that much earlier or the plane was delayed just a few minutes more.

You needn't turn to artificial scenarios like this one to see the effects of counterfactuals. Consider the medalists in the Olympics. Who is happier, the bronze medalist or the silver? You'd think that objectively the silver medalist, who, after all, has actually done better, would be happier. But the relevant counterfactuals are very different for the two. For the bronze medalist the relevant alternative was to finish out of the medals altogether—a fate she has just escaped. For the silver medalist, the relevant alternative was to get the gold medal—a fate she has just missed. And, in fact, when psychologists took clips of the medals ceremonies and analyzed the facial expressions of the athletes, it turned out that the bronze medalists really do look happier than the silver medalists. The difference in what might have been outweighs the difference in what is.

Like Mr. Crane at the airport, or the silver medalist, people are most unhappy when a desirable outcome seems to be just out of reach, or to have just been missed. As Neil Young adapted John Greenleaf Whittier: "The saddest words of tongue and pen are these four words, 'it might have been.'"

Why do we humans worry so much about counterfactuals, when, by definition, they are things that didn't actually happen? Why are these imaginary worlds just as important to us as the real ones? Surely "it is, and it's awful" should be sadder words than "it might have been."

The evolutionary answer is that counterfactuals let us change the future. Because we can consider alternative ways the world might be, we can actually act on the world and intervene to turn it into one or the other of these possibilities. Whenever we act, even in a small way, we are changing the course of history, nudging the world down one path rather than another. Of course, making one possibility come true means that all the other alternative possibilities we considered won't come true—they become counterfactuals. But being able to think about those possibilities is crucial to our evolutionary success. Counterfactual thinking lets us make new plans, invent new tools, and create new environments. Human beings are constantly imagining what would happen if they cracked nuts or wove baskets or made political decisions in a new way, and the sum total of all those visions is a different world.

Counterfactuals about the past, and the characteristically human emotions that go with them, seem to be the price we pay for counterfactuals about the future. Because we are responsible for the future, we can feel guilty about the past; because we can hope, we can also regret; because we can make plans, we can be disappointed. The other side of being able to consider all the possible futures, all the things that could go differently, is that you can't escape considering all the possible pasts, all the things that could have gone differently.

COUNTERFACTUALS IN CHILDREN: PLANNING THE FUTURE

Can children think counterfactually? The most evolutionarily fundamental kind of counterfactual thinking comes when we make plans for the future—when we consider alternative possibilities and pick the one we think will be most desirable. How can we tell if a very young baby can do this? In my lab, we showed the baby the sort of post with stacking rings that is a standard baby toy. But I had taped over the hole in one of the rings. How would the baby respond to this apparently similar but actually recalcitrant ring? When we brought a fifteen-month-old into the lab he would use a kind of trial-and-error method to solve the problem. He would stack some of the rings, look carefully at the taped-over one—and then try it on the post. And then try it on the post again, harder. And try it on the post one more time. Then he would look up puzzled, try one of the other rings again—and then again try the taped-over one. Basically, young babies would keep at this until they gave up.

But as they got older and learned more about how the world worked, babies would behave entirely differently. An eighteen-month-old would stack all the other rings and then hold up the trick ring with a "Who do you think you're kidding?" look and refuse even to try it. Or she would immediately pick the trick ring up and dramatically throw it across the room, and then calmly stack the rest. Or, equally dramatically, she would hold it up to the post and shout "No!" or "Uh-oh!" These babies didn't have to actually see what the ring would do—they could imagine what would happen if you put it on the post, and act accordingly.

In another experiment we saw whether babies could discover a new use for an object—if they could, in a simple way, invent a new tool. I put a desirable toy out of the babies' reach and placed a toy rake beside it. As with the ring, fifteen-month-olds sometimes did pick up the rake, but they couldn't figure out how to use it as a tool. They pushed the toy from side to side or even, frustratingly, farther away from them, till they either accidentally got it or gave up. But older babies looked at the rake and paused thoughtfully. You could almost see the wheels spinning. Then they produced a triumphant smile and often a certain look of smugness.

You could almost see the lightbulb switching on. Then they put the rake in just the right position over the toy and triumphantly used it to bring the toy toward them. Again they seemed able to mentally anticipate—to imagine—all the possible ways the rake could affect the toy and then chose just the right possibility.

Simple trial and error, trying different actions until one succeeds, is actually often a very effective way of getting along in the world. But anticipating future possibilities lets us plan in this other more insightful way—using our heads instead of our hands. The older babies seemed to be anticipating the possible future in which the ring or the rake would fail and avoiding that future. Other studies have shown that this isn't just a difference between fifteen- and eighteen-month-olds. Even younger babies can solve problems insightfully if they have the right kinds of information.

This ability to solve problems insightfully seems to be particularly human. There is a little evidence that chimpanzees, and even some very smart birds like crows, can do this occasionally. But even chimpanzees and crows, and certainly other animals, overwhelmingly rely on either instinct or trial and error to get along in the world. And, in fact, instinct and trial and error are often very effective and intelligent strategies. It is extremely impressive to see a bird putting together the complex set of instinctive behaviors that allows it to build a nest, or a chimpanzee using trial and error to gradually zero in on the right strategy to open a box with elaborate locks. But they are different from the strategies that babies and very young children use. Anthropologists agree that using tools and making plans, both abilities that depend on anticipating future possibilities, played a large role in the evolutionary success of *Homo sapiens*. And we can see these abilities emerging even in babies who can't talk yet.

RECONSTRUCTING THE PAST

In these experiments babies seem to be able to imagine alternative possibilities in the future. Can children also imagine past counterfactuals, different ways the world might have been? We have to infer babies' counterfactual thinking from what they do, but we can explicitly ask older children counterfactual woulda-coulda-shoulda questions. Until recently psychologists claimed that children were quite bad at thinking about possibilities. Children are indeed quite bad at producing counterfactuals about subjects they know little about, but when they understand the subject matter even two- and three-year-olds turn out to be adept at generating alternative worlds.

The English psychologist Paul Harris probably knows more than anyone about young children's imaginative abilities. Harris is tall, thin, reserved, and very English, and worked for many years at Oxford University. His work, like the work of the great Oxford writer Lewis Carroll, is a peculiarly English combination of the strictest logic applied to the wildest fantasy.

Harris told children a familiar English countryside story. Then he asked them about future and past counterfactuals. Naughty Ducky is wearing muddy boots and is about to walk into the kitchen. "What would happen to the floor if Ducky walked through the kitchen? Would it be clean or dirty?" "What would have happened to the floor if Ducky had cleaned his boots first? Would it be clean or dirty?" Even young three-year-olds say that the floor would have been spared if only Ducky had cleaned his boots.

In my lab, David Sobel and I designed a set of storytelling cards—cartoon pictures that told the right story if you put them in order. We showed children a sequence of pictures, say a girl going to a cookie jar, opening the jar, looking inside, finding cookies, and looking happy. But we also had a set of several other pictures, including the girl finding that there were no cookies, and the girl looking sad and hungry. We showed the children the cards in the right sequence and asked them to tell the story. Then we said, "But how about if the girl had been sad at the end instead?" and changed the last card, so that the girl looked sad instead of happy. "What would have had to happen then?" Three-year-olds consistently changed the earlier pictures to fit the hypothetical ending—they replaced the picture of the full cookie jar with the picture of the empty one. These very young children could imagine and reason about an alternative past.

IMAGINING THE POSSIBLE

We can also see evidence for counterfactual thinking in children's play. Babies start pretending when they are as young as eighteen months old or even younger. Pretending involves a kind of present counterfactual thinking—imagining the way things might be different. Even babies who can't talk yet, and are barely walking, can still pretend. A one-and-a-half-year-old baby may fastidiously comb her hair with a pencil, or rest her head on a pillow dramatically pretending to be asleep, giggling all the while. A little later babies start to treat objects as if they were something else. Toddlers turn everything from blocks to shoes to bowls of cereal into means of transportation by the simple expedient of saying "brrm-brrm" and pushing them along the floor. Or they may carefully, tenderly, put three little toy sheep to bed.

We take this for granted when we choose toys for these young children. The toddler sections of toy stores are full of toys that encourage children to pretend: the farmhouse, the gas station, the zoo—even the toy ATM and cell phone. But it's not that two-year-olds pretend because we give them dolls; instead we give them dolls because they love to pretend. Even without toys toddlers are just as likely to turn common objects—food, pebbles, grass, you, themselves—into something else. And even in cultures where pretend play is discouraged, rather than cultivated, like Mr. Gradgrind's school in Dickens's *Hard Times*, children continue to do it anyway. ("No child left behind" testing policies seem to be echoing Mr. Gradgrind, replacing dress-up corners and pretend play with reading drills in preschools.)

As soon as babies can talk they immediately talk about the possible as well as the real. As a graduate student at Oxford I recorded all the words that nine babies used when they first began to talk. These babies, who were still just using single words, at the very start of language, would use them to talk about possibilities as well as actualities. There was not only the ubiquitous "brrm-brrm," but "apple" when pretending to eat a ball, or "night-night" when putting a doll to bed. One particularly charming red-haired toddler had a beloved teddy bear, and his mother had knitted two long scarves, like the ones Dr. Who wears in the British TV series, a small one for the bear and a larger one for Jonathan. Jonathan one day put his teddy bear's scarf around his neck and, with enormous grins and giggles, announced his new identity: "Jonathan Bear!"

In fact, learning language gives children a whole powerful new way to imagine. Even young babies who can't talk yet have some ability to anticipate and imagine the future. But being able to talk gives you a particularly powerful way to put old ideas together in new ways, and to talk about things that aren't there. Consider the power of "no," one of the very first words that children learn. When parents think about "no" they immediately think of the terrible two-year-old absolutely refusing to do something. And children do use "no" that way. But they also use "no" to tell themselves not to do something, like the child who said "no" holding the taped-up ring over the post. And they use "no" to say that something isn't true. When Jonathan's equally charming mom teased him by saying that the swimming pool was full of orange juice, he immediately said, "No juice!" Other less obvious words have some of the same power. Take "uh-oh." This hardly counts as a word for grown-ups but it's one of the most common words that young children use. And "uh-oh," like "no," is a word about what could have happened. Babies use it when they try to do something and fail—"uh-oh" contrasts the ideal with the unfortunate real.

Being able to say "no" and "uh-oh" immediately puts you in the world of the counterfactual and the possible—the road not taken, the possibility that isn't real. And we discovered that, in fact, babies start talking about unreal possibilities at the same time that they start to use tools in an insightful way. Being able to talk about possibilities helps you to imagine them.

By the time they are two or three children quite characteristically spend much of their waking hours in a world of imaginary creatures, possible universes, and assumed identities. Walk into any day-care center and you will be surrounded by small princesses and superheroes in overalls who politely serve you nonexistent tea and warn you away from nonexistent monsters. And these children are adept at playing out the consequences of their counterfactual pretend premises. Paul Harris found that even two-year-olds will tell you that if an imaginary teddy is drinking imaginary tea, then if he spills it the imaginary floor will require imaginary mopping-up. (As with Ducky, toddlers seem particularly taken with the possibilities involved in making a terrible mess.) Children were quite specific about their counterfactuals. If the teddy spills tea you'll need a mop, but if he spills baby powder you'll need a broom.

In the past, this imaginative play has been taken to be evidence of children's cognitive limitations rather than evidence of their cognitive powers. Earlier psychologists, including both Freud and Piaget, claimed that make-believe was a sign that young children are unable to discriminate between fiction and truth, pretense and reality, fantasy and fact. Of course, if you saw an adult doing the same things that preschoolers do—if, for example, someone with wild hair and a sparkly cloak around her shoulders announced to you that she was queen of the fairies—you would probably conclude that she *was* confused about reality and fantasy, and that she should probably make sure she got back on her meds. However, neither Freud nor Piaget investigated this question systematically.

More recently, cognitive scientists have carefully explored what children know about imagination and pretense. It turns out that even two- and three-year-olds are extremely good at distinguishing imagination and pretense from reality. One of the most distinctive things about even the earliest pretend play is the fact that it's accompanied by giggles. It's the giggles, the knowing look, the dramatic exaggeration, that signal that this is not to be taken seriously. In fact, there turns out to be a consistent set of signals—giggles, exaggerated gestures, theatrical and melodramatic facial expressions—that indicate that actions are "just pretend." And, after all, even the youngest children don't actually try to eat the pretend cookies or even try to actually talk to Mom on the pretend cell phone.

Preschool children spend hours pretending, but they *know* that they are pretending. The psychologist Jacqui Woolley did an experiment where children pretended that there was a pencil in one box, and actually saw a pencil in another box. Then the boxes were closed. An assistant came into the room, looking for a pencil, and asked the children which box she should open. Three-year-olds said quite clearly that she should look in the box with the real pencil, not the pretend one. In much the same way three-year-olds say that everyone can see and touch a real dog but not an imaginary one, and that you can turn an imaginary dog, but not a real one, into a cat just by thinking about it.

Children may seem confused because they are such expressive and emotional pretenders. They can have real emotional reactions to entirely imaginary scenarios. Rather than asking children to imagine pencils in the box, Paul Harris asked them to imagine a monster in the box. Children again said very clearly that really there was no monster in the box, and that they would not see one if they opened the box—they were just imagining it. Nevertheless, when the experimenter left the room many children gingerly moved away from the box.

In this respect, however, children don't seem to be that different from adults. The psychologist Paul Rozin asked adults to fill a bottle with water from the tap, write "cyanide" on a label, and affix it to the bottle. Although they knew perfectly well that they were only pretending that the water was poisonous, they still wouldn't drink it. I am perfectly capable of being scared silly by Hannibal Lecter although I have absolutely no doubt of his fictional status.

Children's emotions are more intense and more difficult to control than adult emotions, whether the causes of those emotions are real or not. To a worried parent, it may seem that the child trembling under the covers must believe that there really is a monster in the closet. But the scientific studies show that this is not because children don't understand the difference between fiction and fact. They are just more moved by both than grown-ups.

IMAGINATION AND CAUSATION

We know that even very young children constantly think about future, past, and present possible worlds. And we know that this ability gives us distinctive evolutionary advantages. How do human minds, even the very youngest human minds, manage to produce counterfactuals? How can we think about the possible worlds that might exist in the future or could have existed in the past, when those worlds don't actually exist now? Even more important, our evolutionary advantage comes because we can not only imagine possibilities but also act on them—we can turn them into reality. But how do we know which possibilities will come true in what circumstances? And how do we decide just what we have to do to make them real?

Part of the answer is that our ability to imagine possible worlds is closely tied to our ability to think causally. Causal knowledge is itself an ancient philosophical puzzle. The great Scottish philosopher David Hume thought we could never really know that one event caused another—all we could know was that one event tended to follow another. What makes causal knowledge more than just one damned thing after another? The modern philosopher David Lewis was the first to point out the close link between causal knowledge and counterfactual thinking, and many philosophers have followed this idea up since then.

Once you know how one thing is causally connected to another you can predict what will happen to one thing if you act to change another—you can see what a difference making things different will make. You can also imagine what would have happened if you had acted in a certain way, even though you didn't. Once I know that smoking causes cancer I can imagine possible worlds in which my actions cause people to stop smoking, and conclude that in those worlds they will be less likely to become ill. I can take a wide variety of actions, from advertising to legislation to inventing nicotine patches, to get people to stop smoking, and I can accurately predict just how these actions will change the world. I can make a world with less cancer than the world had before. And

I can also look backwards and calculate how many lives would have been saved if the tobacco industry had not resisted those changes in the past.

Causal understanding lets you deliberately do things that will change the world in a particular way. We might simply have had the ability to track the world as it unfolded around us. But, in fact, we have the ability to intervene in the world, as well, to actually make things happen. Intervening deliberately in the world isn't the same as just predicting what will happen next. When we intervene we envision a particular possible future we would like to bring about and our action actually changes the world to make that future real.

Of course, other animals, or people in some situations, may act on the world effectively without necessarily understanding the world in a causal way. Like the fifteen-month-olds and the ring, or like the chimpanzees, you may just hit on the right action to solve a problem through trial and error. Chimpanzees may notice that when you poke a stick in a termite nest, the termites emerge. Fifteen-month-olds may see that when you try the taped-over ring it fails, and doctors may observe that when you prescribe aspirin your patient's headaches go away. Then you can just repeat that action the next time.

But having a causal theory of the world makes it possible to consider alternative solutions to a problem, and their consequences, before you actually implement them, and it lets you make a much wider and more effective range of interventions. If you know that the hole allows the ring to descend on the post, or that the rake causes the toy to move with it, you can design a new strategy to deal with the taped-over ring or the distant toy. If you know that a cascade of electrical impulses on the trigeminal nerve leads the blood vessels to expand, which puts pressure on nerves, which leads to a headache, you can design drugs that influence just the electrical processes or just the blood pressure. When you take a drug like sumatriptan to relieve a migraine headache you are taking advantage of the causal knowledge about migraines that neurologists have discovered, and the possible remedies that it allowed them to design.

CHILDREN AND CAUSATION

Understanding what causes migraines and cancer, and using this knowledge to change the world, is, of course, the work of science. But are scientists the only people who can think about causation and use it to bring new worlds into being? Ordinary adults also seem to know a lot about the causal structure of the world and they irresistibly think about counterfactuals, even when all they do is lead to guilt and regret.

We saw that children are also extremely good at counterfactual thinking. If counterfactual thinking depends on causal understanding and is a deep, evolved part of human nature, then even very young children should also be able to think causally. In fact, it turns out that they do already know a great deal about the causal structure of the world—about how one thing makes another happen. In fact, this is one of the most important, and most revolutionary, recent discoveries of developmental psychology.

Just as psychologists used to think that children don't understand much about counterfactuals, they also used to think that young children don't understand much about causation. Children's thinking was supposed to be restricted to their immediate perceptual experience—they might know that one event happened after another but not that one event caused another. In particular, psychologists thought that children didn't understand the hidden causal relations that are the stuff of science—the way that something in a seed makes it grow, or germs make you ill, or magnets make iron filings move, or hidden desires make people act. Piaget, for example, claimed that children were "precausal" until they were well into the school-age years.

But over the past twenty years we have discovered that babies and young children do know a lot about how objects and people work, and they learn more as they grow older.

Piaget asked children about causal phenomena that they didn't know much about. He asked preschoolers interesting and hard causal questions like "Why does it get dark at night?" or "Why do the clouds move?" The children either simply got confused or produced answers that were deficient by adult standards though they sometimes had a logic of their own ("It gets dark so we can sleep" or "The clouds move because I want them to").

More recently psychologists decided to try asking children questions about things they know a lot about, like "Why did Johnny open the refrigerator when he was hungry?" or "How does a tricycle work?" Children as young as two gave perfectly good, and sometimes even elaborate, causal explanations. "He thought there was food in there and he wanted food so he opened the fridge so he could get the food." Very young children are consumed with insatiable curiosity about causes, as their unstoppable "why?" questions show.

The psychologist Henry Wellman spent a sabbatical year simply searching through CHILDES, a computer database of recordings of hundreds of children's everyday conversations. (Wellman, who once taught preschool, said that it was odd and touching to simultaneously be in the scholarly adult peace of the computer room at the Center for Advanced Studies in the Behavioral Sciences at Stanford and yet be surrounded once more by these invisible

three-year-olds.) He found that two- and three-year-olds both produced and asked for dozens of causal explanations a day. They
gave explanations for physical phenomena: "The teddy's arm fell
off because you twisted it too far"; "Jenny had my chair because
the other chair was brokened." They gave accounts of biological
causes: "He needs more to eat because he is growing long arms";
"Mean hawks eat meat because meat is tasty for mean hawks."
But most of all they liked psychological explanations: "I didn't spill
it last night because I'm a good girl"; "I not gone go up there because I frightened of her." The explanations might not always have
been the same ones a grown-up would give but they were perfectly
good logical explanations all the same.

Other studies show that young children understand quite abstract and hidden causes. They understand that something in a
seed makes it grow or that invisible germs make you ill. The Japanese psychologists Giyoo Hatano and Kayoko Inagaki explored
children's everyday biology—their understanding of life and death.
They found that when they're around five years old children around
the world develop a vitalist causal theory of biology, much like the
theory in traditional Japanese and Chinese medicine. These children seem to think that there is a single vital force, like the Chi-
nese chi, that keeps us alive. They predict that if you don't eat
enough, for example, this force will wane and you'll get sick. They
think that death is the irreversible loss of this force, and predict
that animals that die won't come back to life. (This new understanding of mortality is a mixed blessing. Younger children think
that death is more like a move than an ending; Grandmom has
simply temporarily taken up residence in the cemetery or in
heaven, and might come back. Many children start to become
much more anxious about death once they think of it as the irre-

versible loss of a vital force.) This theory allows them to make a whole network of predictions, counterfactuals, and explanations— like the child Henry Wellman studied who said that someone "needs more to eat because he is growing long arms."

Causation is what gives fantasy its logic. Think about the children in Paul Harris's studies who could work out precisely what the imaginary consequences would be if Teddy spilled the imaginary tea. A pretend game in which absolutely anything goes would just be a mess. Instead, pretend works by establishing imaginary premises ("I'm the mommy and you're the baby") and then working out the causal consequences of those premises quite strictly. Children can become quite passionate about whether the right causal rules are being followed: "You didn't get me with your ray gun 'cause I was behind the shield!" "You hafta drink your milk 'cause you're the baby!"

CAUSES AND POSSIBILITIES

Children develop causal theories of the world from a very early age. If causal knowledge and counterfactual thinking go together, then this might explain how young children have the parallel ability to generate counterfactuals and to explore possible worlds. If children understand the way things work, they should be able to imagine alternative possibilities about them. This might also explain the cases where children don't think counterfactually. Think back to the fifteen-month-old who futilely tries to jam the solid ring over the pole. It could be that she just doesn't understand yet how poles and holes fit together. Children might sometimes fail to think counterfactually because they don't have the right kind of causal knowledge, not because they're unable to imagine possibilities, just as I would have a hard time telling you what could have been done to prevent the space shuttle crash, or what should be done to prevent it in the future.

Henry Wellman showed that children talk about causes in their everyday conversations. Then he took the next step and asked children to say what was possible or impossible, based on their causal knowledge of the physical, biological, and psychological world. He found that children consistently used their knowledge to discriminate possibilities. They said, for example, that Johnny could simply decide to hold up his arm, but he couldn't possibly decide to simply jump in the air and stay there, or decide to grow taller, or decide to walk through a table.

One little boy we tested decided to demonstrate his counterfactual knowledge by actually acting out each of the possibilities after he had made the predictions. "You can't just jump in the air and stay there, look!" he said, jumping as high as he could. And then: "Watch! Table I will walk through you!" at which he dramatically and theatrically bumped against the table and said, "Ow, see, you can't do it."

Even the youngest children already have causal knowledge about the world and use that knowledge to make predictions about the future, to explain the past, and to imagine possible worlds that might or might not exist. But at a deeper level, what would children's minds have to be like in order to do this? One way Wellman, Hatano and Inagaki, and I tried to capture these ideas was by saying that children have everyday theories of the world—everyday ideas about psychology, biology, and physics. These theories are like scientific theories but they are largely unconscious rather than conscious, and they are coded in children's brains, instead of being written down on paper or presented at sci-

their specific information about routes through the Misty Mountains and the exact distance between Osgiliath and Mordor. The map of Middle-earth uses exactly the same resources as the map of your local town, or the garden plan, but it allows you to imagine a fictional space rather than understand a real space or create a new one. In just the same way, we can use the apparatus of causal thinking to construct fictional counterfactuals as well as past and future counterfactuals.

The line between a fiction and a counterfactual is one of degree rather than kind. Fictions are counterfactuals that just happen to be further away from our real world than other possible worlds. A fiction is a counterfactual out there where the buses don't run. If past counterfactuals are the price we pay for future counterfactuals, then fictional counterfactuals are the free bonus we get. Because we can plan, hope, and be responsible for the future we can also wonder, daydream, and escape into the fictional.

WHY MINDS AND THINGS ARE DIFFERENT

The research shows that children's imaginary companions are linked to what they learn about other people. Children pretend so much because they are learning so much. And this early pretending seems to be continuous with adult fiction. This may help to explain an apparent conundrum. Why is it that, even for adults, the transparent lies of fiction seem mysteriously able to convey deep truths about the human condition? Why do plays and novels, poems and stories and myths, mean so much to us? Why is it that even a professional scientific psychologist like me feels that I've learned more about human personality and social life from Jane Austen than from the *Journal of Personality and Social Psychology*?

There are some important differences between causal maps of

the physical world and those of the psychological world. Just as maps of the physical world allow us to change that world, so do maps of the psychological world. But in the psychological case there is an even more intimate relation between causes and counterfactuals, maps and blueprints. To intervene in the physical world we need a lot of cooperation from the causal structure of that world. It may take years or even centuries to figure out the technology to build a bridge or dam a stream.

It seems to be much easier to intervene on minds, including our own minds. We can use our words, as they say in preschool. There is something almost supernatural about psychological causation—say a few words from across the room or even across the country and you can instantly make someone else sigh with love or boil with anger. Or think about the way that a single e-mail announcing a meeting can cause people from all over the world to move to exactly the same spot at the same time. Doing the same thing to rocks or trees would seem like magic.

In fact, just about everything in the psychological world is shaped by human intervention. We can, of course, change the physical world in quite radical ways and very "unnatural" physical worlds will result. Most of the physical structure of any modern city is the result of human intervention. But we can at least contrast this with physical worlds that have not been altered by human intervention (though we may soon have to go to Mars or the moon to do so).

In the psychological case there is no "natural" world, no unspoiled mental wilderness. Even hunter-gatherer cultures are shaped by the particular conventions, traditions, and intentions of their members. The Warlpiri Australian aborigines are just as different from the Baka pygmies of Africa as urban Americans are from urban Japanese. A wild animal or a wildflower is fully an animal or a flower. But a wild child, like the famous Wild Child of Aveyron, is a damaged and injured child.

The range of imaginative possibilities in the psychological world also seems wider than the range in the physical world, and the constraints seem to be less strong. The extraordinary variety of human cultures is testimony to that. Of course, there are some psychological universals. All humans have beliefs, desires, and emotions, are happy when their desires are fulfilled and unhappy when they are not, and so on. Not every psychological arrangement is possible, and evolutionary psychologists may be right to suggest that some arrangements are harder to sustain than others. It may be an evolutionary fact that we humans have a hard time maintaining monogamy or celibacy, but it is equally an evolutionary fact, and a more surprising and interesting one, that we humans can and do invent monogamy or celibacy, or democracy, or sexual equality or pacifism or any number of other brand-new psychological attitudes (not to mention the psychological states that constitute being a tea ceremony adept, a Deadhead, or a Cubs fan). The celibate or the Cubs fan actually takes on the desires and beliefs that come with that role, even if the desire not to have sex or the faith that the Cubs will win may seem highly irrational from an evolutionary point of view. To understand what the celibate or the Cubs fan does you have to understand those "unnatural" desires and beliefs.

As a result, it is often very difficult to tell whether children are learning about the causal structure of other people's minds or changing their own minds. An American child learns what American minds are like, and a Japanese child learns what Japanese minds are like, just as they learn what American and Japanese tables and chairs and landscapes are like. But, simultaneously, that learning seems to allow the child, indeed to invite her, to make her mind into an American or Japanese one. Does the child simply discover that the people around her value individuality more than cooperation? Or does that discovery make her become somebody who values individuality more than cooperation herself?

For all these reasons, in the psychological case it is hard to separate the maps and the blueprints. Many of the most central causal facts about other people, the facts about them we most need to know to predict and change what they will do, are the result of some past history of human intervention. What we do and think always reflects what other people have said and done to us, and even more significantly what we have said and done to ourselves.

But it is important to see that there is nothing mystical, or relativist, or antievolutionary about this. We, and those around us, may create our psychological worlds more than we discover them, and discover our physical worlds more than we create them, but the same distinctive human reasoning is involved in both cases. The causal maps in our minds allow us both to understand the existing physical and psychological worlds and to invent and realize new physical and psychological worlds. They simultaneously let us make predictions, imagine alternative possibilities, and create fictions.

SOUL ENGINEERS

In the physical case, our causal maps, our theories, seem to be primary, and the engineering applications of those maps, the blueprints, seem to follow after. And while there certainly are fictional physical counterfactuals—in science fiction, for example, we may imagine different ways that the physical world could work—they're less pervasive and compelling than psychological fictions.

In the psychological case the counterfactuals, the blueprints and fictions, seem especially important. A great work of fiction presents us with a blueprint of the many ways we and others could choose to be (or not to be), and a kind of outline of the causal consequences of those choices. It tells us about the ways that people might be. Lady Murasaki tells us something new about the possible ways to love, as Proust tells us about snobbery, or Homer tells us about heroism. The writer Joseph Škvorecký, quoting Josef Stalin, of all people, said that novelists were the engineers of human souls—and this may quite literally be true.

Children work out the imaginary consequences if Teddy spills the imaginary tea, or if you try to have lunch with Charlie Ravioli, or get into the crib with Dunzer. Writers work out the imaginary consequences of Genji's imaginary charisma or Marcel's imaginary social climbing or Achilles' imaginary pride.

The child who works through the tragicomic story of Teddy's tea tells us that he understands teddies and teapots. The charm of the story of Charlie Ravioli is that three-year-old Olivia had already figured out the peculiar causal structure of busy New York literary life. She knew that if you bump into somebody in the street, the right thing to say is "Let's have lunch sometime" and even that leaving messages on a busy person's answering machine is unlikely to be effective. Though she was only three, she'd taken all her individual experiences of New York life and turned them into a single coherent theory of New York. By telling the story of Charlie Ravioli, Olivia conveyed just how much she knew about how that particular New York psychology worked. Her laid-back California cousins could work out what that life must be like, just by listening, even though they had no firsthand experience of yellow cabs and corner coffee shops.

The stories of Genji, Marcel, and Achilles convey more sophisticated adult psychological knowledge—a kind of knowledge that we might not have had until we read the book. Just as we could work out what twenty-first-century literary New York must be like from Olivia's story, we can work out what eleventh-century Japanese life, or nineteenth-century French life, or ancient Greek life was like from theirs. More, we can discover aspects of our own lives that are also implicit in those stories.

W. H. Auden, reviewing *The Lord of the Rings* when it first came out, pointed to the apparent conflict between the superficial unreality, not to say silliness, of much of the book—those awful Orcs and twee elves—and its simultaneous deep appeal. Auden said that all lives viewed from the outside, as we might view a physical sequence of events, were like a certain kind of grim realist fiction—one boring, somewhat depressing thing after another. But, he went on, all lives viewed from the inside are a matter of choices, selecting a path among many counterfactual possibilities, making one's way through many possible worlds. Even in the most commonplace life, trivial goals become imbued with the overwhelming importance and significance that is necessary to initiate action, while ordinary frustrations become mountains and chasms. From the inside, from the psychological perspective, any human life takes on the structure of a possibly hopeless but crucially important quest against overwhelmingly daunting obstacles. Fictional counterfactuals, even wildly fictional ones like *The Lord of the Rings*, help provide maps and guides for that sort of journey.

THE WORK OF PLAY

Even the youngest children ubiquitously create fictions in much the same way that adult writers and readers do. The curious thing about children's pretense, though, is that children actively seek out the wild fictive counterfactuals that are cognitive lagniappe for adults.

From the adult perspective, the fictional worlds are a luxury. It's the future predictions that are the real deal, the stern and earnest stuff of adult life. For young children, however, the imaginary worlds seem just as important and appealing as the real ones. It's not, as scientists used to think, that children can't tell the difference between the real world and the imaginary world. (Recall that the children in Harris's and Taylor's experiments knew very well that the pretend monster or the imaginary companion wasn't real.) It's just that they don't see any particular reason for preferring to live in the real one.

When we see our children immersed in their pretend worlds we say, "Oh, she's playing." This is very revealing. In adult life we distinguish between useful activities, such as cooking dinner or building bridges, and activities such as reading novels and going to the movies, that are just, as we say, "fun" or "entertainment"—in other words, play. Since young children are protected from the pressures of everyday life, since they are, to be blunt, completely useless, everything they do looks like play. They aren't out building bridges and plowing fields and they don't make dinner or bring home a paycheck. And yet their obsessive and unstoppable pretend play—that parade of fictional counterfactuals—reflects the most sophisticated, important, and characteristic human abilities.

This apparently useless behavior may be very functional from a broader evolutionary perspective. Think about the evolutionary picture I outlined in the first chapter. There is a kind of division of labor between our young selves and our older selves. Our young selves get to freely explore both this world, and all the possible counterfactual worlds, without worrying about which of those worlds will actually turn out to be inhabitable. We adults are the ones who have to figure out whether we want to move into one of those possible worlds, and how to drag all our furniture in there too.

While children may be useless, they are useless on purpose. Because, as children, we don't have to restrict our imaginings to the immediately useful, we can freely construct causal maps and exercise our ability to create counterfactuals. We can compute a wide range of possibilities, not just the two or three that are most likely to pay off. We can consider different ways the world might be, not just the ways the world actually is. As adults our causal maps of the physical and psychological world, and our ability to consider other ways the world might be, will let us conquer the stern and earnest universe of future possibilities.

This division of labor may lead to other differences between adults and children. I mentioned earlier that one of the clearest differences between babies and young children on one hand, and older children and adults on the other, is what psychologists call the development of inhibition—the ability to keep yourself from acting impulsively. Inhibition lets us avoid doing what we feel like immediately, in the service of our larger goals. The commonplace that babies and young children are uninhibited compared with adults is literally true, and we even have some ideas about the brain changes in the prefrontal cortex that lead to those changes in inhibition.

Usually psychologists act as if this childish uninhibitedness is a defect. And, of course, if your agenda is to figure out how to get along well in the everyday world—how to actually do things effectively—it is a defect. But if your agenda is simply to explore both the actual world and all the possible worlds, this apparent defect may be a great asset. Pretend play is notably uninhibited; young children just can't help themselves from following up any random imaginative thought. And young children, unlike adults, don't seem to prefer the close counterfactuals of planning to the distant counterfactuals of fiction. They don't choose to explore only the possibilities that might be useful—they explore all the possibilities.

The evolutionary outcome of this uninhibited exploration is that children can learn more than adults can. But children aren't wild pretenders because they are consciously trying to learn about the world or other people. They are wild pretenders because they are children and that's what children do. It's only from the broader evolutionary perspective that their uninhibited useless pretense turns out to be among the most deeply functional human activities.

Adult fiction sits between the wildly uninhibited counterfactuals of childhood and the sternly practical ones of adulthood. One way of thinking about adult fiction writers is that they combine the cognitive freedom of childhood with the discipline of adulthood. Adult dramatists, unlike most adults and like children, are exploring the possibilities of human experience for their own sake. But unlike children, and like their fellow adults, they do this on purpose and with the dedication and discipline that all adult endeavors require.

The idea that art and literature reflect our capacity for play is not new, of course, but thinking about the cognitive role of children's play gives this old idea a new force. The wild, harebrained, uninhibited three-year-old may be quite unable to do something as simple as get her snowsuit on (there are so many distractions: she has to play with the imaginary tiger and make sure her imaginary friend is dressed too). But she is, in fact, exercising some of the most sophisticated and philosophically profound capacities of human nature—though admittedly that may be cold comfort to the parent who has to make it to work on time.

3.
Escaping Plato's Cave

HOW CHILDREN, SCIENTISTS, AND COMPUTERS

DISCOVER THE TRUTH

*

S ocrates is talking to Glaucon:

Behold! human beings living in a underground den, which has a mouth open towards the light and reaching all along the den; here they have been from their childhood, and have their legs and necks chained so that they cannot move, and can only see before them, being prevented by the chains from turning round their heads. Above and behind them a fire is blazing at a distance, and between the fire and the prisoners there is a raised way; and you will see, if you look, a low wall built along the way, like the screen which marionette players have in front of them, over which they show the puppets.

I see.

And do you see, I said, men passing along the wall carrying all sorts of vessels, and statues and figures of animals made of wood and stone and various materials, which appear over the wall? Some of them are talking, others silent.

You have shown me a strange image, and they are strange prisoners.

Like ourselves, I replied; and they see only their own shadows, or the shadows of one another, which the fire throws on the opposite wall of the cave?

True, he said; how could they see anything but the shadows if they were never allowed to move their heads?

And of the objects which are being carried in like manner they would only see the shadows?

Yes, he said.

And if they were able to converse with one another, would they not suppose that they were naming what was actually before them?

Very true.

And suppose further that the prison had an echo which came from the other side, would they not be sure to fancy when one of the passers-by spoke that the voice which they heard came from the passing shadow?

No question, he replied.

To them, I said, the truth would be literally nothing but the shadows of the images.

—*from Plato's* Republic

Socrates' point, of course, is that we are these prisoners. This famous, ancient picture, the chained prisoners in the smoky cave, is still a compellingly creepy statement of one of the oldest philosophical problems. *The Matrix* used much the same image with the same impact, though with more elaborate special effects. All that reaches us from the world are a few rays of light hitting our retinas, and a few air molecules vibrating at our eardrums—images and echoes. So how can we really know anything about the outside world? Where do our theories of the world come from and how do we get them right?

Developmental psychologists have known for a long time that babies and children are prodigious learners. Some of us even have suggested that children use the same powerful learning techniques that scientists use. However, we didn't know very much in detail about how this learning was possible—either for scientists or children. In fact, I thought that this was a problem that would not be solved in my lifetime—but I was wrong. In the last few years we've made amazing progress in understanding how at least some kinds of learning are possible and how scientists and babies can accurately discover the truth about the world around them.

In the last two chapters we saw that even very young children know about the causal structure of the world. They make causal maps. This knowledge gives them remarkable abilities to imagine alternative worlds and to change this one. And these causal maps develop: five-year-olds know more than three-year-olds, who know more than one-year-olds. Children's causal maps get better—they represent the world more and more accurately, and this allows the children to imagine more powerfully and to act more effectively. Children are correctly learning how the world works. So babies must be born with powerful causal learning mechanisms.

But even if we know that these causal learning mechanisms must be in place, can we say anything more about what they're like and how they could allow us to grasp the truth? Causal learning is a notorious example of the gap between experience and truth. The great philosopher David Hume originally articulated the difficulty: "where we have observed a single event followed by another, we are not entitled to form a general rule or foretell what will happen in like cases, it being justly esteemed an unpardonable temerity . . . And there is nothing in a number of instances different from every single instance."

All we see are contingencies between events—one event follows another. How do we ever know that one event actually caused the other? And the problem gets worse. In real life, causal relations rarely involve just two events. Instead, dozens of different events are related in complicated ways. And in real life, it's actually rare for one event to *always* follow another. Usually, the cause just makes the effect more likely, not absolutely certain. Smoking causes lung cancer, but not always, and whether a particular smoker actually gets cancer depends on a complex web of other factors.

Like any good philosophical problem, the problem of causal learning is still far from completely solved, but there's been a lot of progress. The same philosophers of science and computer scientists who worked out the mathematics of causal maps also worked out techniques for learning those maps. They developed a mathematical account of how an ideal scientist could learn about causes. And they've started to turn that abstract mathematics into real computer programs, programs that can actually learn about the world.

These programs depend on the logic and mathematics of probability. When we think about logic, we usually think in terms of cut-and-dried certainties, absolute answers. But in science, and in ordinary life, we don't get those kinds of answers. The accumulated evidence may make some possibilities more or less likely, but it rarely gives us certainties.

However, to say that there is no absolute answer doesn't mean that there is no answer at all. In fact, we can be quite certain about uncertainties, and quite precise about imprecise knowledge—we can formulate a kind of probabilistic logic. Much of the recent work takes off from ideas about probability that were first formulated by the philosopher, mathematician, and theologian Reverend Thomas Bayes back in the eighteenth century. Bayes's published work, with titles such as *Divine Benevolence; or, An Attempt to Prove That the Principal End of the Divine Providence and Government Is the Happiness of His Creatures*, is long forgotten, but the unpublished essay on probability that was found in his papers after he died has become the foundation for much of twenty-first-century computer science and artificial intelligence. (In a search for Bayes on the net, the *Encyclopedia of Philosophy* article was followed by a commercial site that advertised Bayesian methods for fixing cars and winning government contracts.)

Rev. Bayes's big idea was that learning is about the probabilities of possibilities. For Bayes nothing is ever certain; instead we just think that some possibilities are more likely than others. As we get more evidence about how the world works we systematically update the likelihood of all those possibilities. A little evidence can nudge one hypothesis just a bit past another one. If the evidence is strong enough even the most unlikely possibility can turn out to be true. Learning is a long, slow process with many false starts and revolutions; things we once thought were hardly possible at all turn out to be true (or at least the best account at the moment). Bayesianism gives you precise mathematical ways to get closer and closer to the truth, even if you don't ever entirely reach it.

Combining Bayesian learning ideas with the causal maps I described in the last chapter has turned out to give computer scientists an extraordinarily powerful way of constructing learning machines. In fact, causal graphical models are often called "Bayes nets." Suppose I have two different possible theories about the world—two possible causal maps. How can I decide which one is actually right?

Recall that the maps let you make predictions. With a map I can say that some outcomes are likelier to happen than others. If I think that smoking causes cancer I can predict that preventing smoking will lower the probability of cancer. If it doesn't cause cancer—if the causal map is different—then preventing smoking won't have this effect. Then I can do an experiment or clinical trial or even just a big epidemiological study and find out what actually happens.

If the map predicted that evidence, then the probability that that is the right map will go up. The new evidence will make one map more likely than another: if the probability of cancer goes down when people stop smoking, the probability that smoking causes cancer goes up. Causal maps give you a way to make predictions about what the world will be like. By comparing those predictions with what actually happens, you can figure out systematically how likely it is that any particular causal map is actually true.

The famous Turing test proposes that you sit at a computer terminal and try to figure out whether you are interacting with a computer or another person. Turing, who invented the modern computer, said that if you can't tell the difference, you will have to grant that the computer has a mind. Servers like Hotmail now do real Turing tests, like asking a user to recognize a blurry word, to make sure they don't give e-mail addresses to spammers' computers. But to be truly convincing a Turing test would have to be more stringent. In his original paper Turing also argued for a "child computer" test. The computer should be able to do the same things as a human adult, but it should also be able to learn how to do those things like a human child.

Computers are far from passing that Turing test, but they're getting a lot better. The new Bayesian ideas let us build computers that can actually learn about the world. Computer scientists working for NASA have begun to design programs that can let a robot learn about the mineral composition of rocks on Mars, without having to consult Earthbound experts. Biostatisticians are designing programs that can take masses of genetic data and learn about the complex causal sequence of events that turns a genome into an organism. NASA scientists are even designing programs that can take satellite data and figure out how the temperature of the ocean off Latin America causes monsoons in India.

These programs work by mimicking the procedures of science. How do scientists solve the problem of causal learning? They use three techniques. They can do statistical analyses of evidence, they can learn from their own experiments, and they can learn from the experiments of others. If I'm a doctor and I want to know if smoking causes cancer, I can analyze the epidemiological data about cancer rates in smokers, I can design a randomized controlled experiment—say, getting half a group of patients to stop smoking, and letting the other half continue—and I can read the journals and find out what experiments everyone else has done. Ideally, I'd do all three. At first glance, these ways of learning about the world seem very complex and abstract. And, in fact, when ordinary adults have to consciously analyze statistics, or design experiments, or evaluate the experiments of others, they usually have a miserable time. Anyone who has taught, or taken, an introductory statistics course can testify to that.

Often, though, people can do things intuitively that they can't do consciously. When we drive, we are unconsciously making very complicated computations about the speed of the car, the effects of the steering wheel, and the nature of the road. When we understand sentences we are unconsciously making very complicated computations about sounds and syntax. It turns out that even the youngest children can use statistics and experiments to learn about the world, in much the way that the sophisticated scientists and NASA computers can.

OBSERVATION: BABY STATISTICS

In statistics we calculate the probabilities of various combinations of events and then use that information to draw causal conclusions. For instance, we can count up the number of smokers and nonsmokers who do or don't get lung cancer. Then we can calculate how likely it is that people who smoke will get cancer and compare that to the likelihood that people who don't smoke will get cancer. Then we factor out other measures such as age and income to show that the link between cancer and smoking isn't due to other causes. With enough information like this we can eventually conclude that smoking causes cancer.

In 1996, in a groundbreaking paper in *Science*, Jenny Saffran showed that even babies as young as eight months old were sensitive to statistical patterns. This paper launched a flood of exciting research about babies' statistical learning abilities.

How could we possibly show that babies can do statistics? Saffran looked at how they learn words. Suppose, for example, you hear the words "pretty baby." When we hear someone say words, as opposed to reading them on the printed page, there aren't actually any pauses, the words just follow one another continuously. (This becomes vivid when you try listening to a foreign language.) So "pretty baby" actually sounds like "prettybaby." How do you know that "pretty" and "baby" are words and "tyba" is not?

If you have listened to English for eight months (especially if you have a typically fond and sappy mom) you will often have heard "pre" followed by "ty" (not only in "pretty baby" but in "pretty boy" and "pretty darling"), and "ba" followed by "by" (not only in "pretty baby" but in "darling baby" and "angel baby"). But you will have heard "ty" followed by "ba" much less often. You might use that probabilistic information ("ty" often follows "pre" but "ba" rarely follows "ty") to figure out that "pre" and "ty" go together but "ty" and "ba" don't.

To see if babies do this, Saffran used a technique for trying to understand infant minds, habituation, in a very clever experiment. Habituation depends on the idea that babies prefer to look at or listen to new things instead of old ones. If you play babies the same kind of sound over and over again, for example, they get bored and turn away from the sound. Play them something new and they become attentive and start listening and turning to the sound again.

You can use this technique to see whether babies are sensitive to statistics. For example, you can play them long strings of nonsense syllables without pauses in various combinations. In one string "ga" is always preceded by "ba," but "da" can follow many different syllables, including "ba." So if you hear "ba" you will definitely hear "ga" next, but there is only a one-third chance that you will hear "da." Then you can play the baby different nonsense "words" in isolation, like, for instance, "bada" or "baga." Remember that babies prefer to listen to things that are new rather than things that are familiar. Will they recognize that "bada" is more unusual than "baga" and prefer to listen to that combination of sounds? They do, as the babies can unconsciously use the pattern of probabilities to figure out which syllables are likely to occur together.

Is this ability to detect probability patterns limited only to language? People such as Steven Pinker or Noam Chomsky would argue that there are very specialized parts of the brain designed just for dealing with language. But eight-month-olds can also detect patterns of probability when you do the same experiment with musical tones (if you hear E followed by D, then C is likely to follow D, the beginning of music appreciation) or with visual scenes (like figuring out that when you see a door you'll also often see a window nearby).

In a particularly dramatic recent study, Fei Xu at the University of British Columbia showed that even nine-month-olds understand some important statistical ideas. She showed babies a transparent box full of mixed-up red and white Ping-Pong balls. Sometimes the balls were mostly white with a few red ones mixed in, sometimes they were mostly red with a few white ones. Then she covered the sides of the box to hide the balls. The experimenter took five balls out of the now opaque box in succession, either four red and one white one or vice versa. If you think about it, it should be surprising, though of course possible, that you just happen to pull mostly red balls out of a mostly white box. It could happen but it's not very likely, and certainly much less likely than pulling out mostly white balls.

Very young babies seemed to reason about probabilities in the same way. They looked longer at the experimenter when she pulled out mostly red balls from a mostly white box than when she pulled out mostly white balls from a mostly white box, or mostly red balls from a mostly red box. Like Reverend Bayes, these nine-month-olds could consider the probabilities of possibilities.

So even nine-month-olds detect the patterns of probability that are the basic data of statistics. Will they use those patterns to draw conclusions about what causes what, in the way that scientists do? At least by the time they are two and a half, and probably earlier, children can also use probabilities to make genuinely causal inferences.

To test this we went back to the blicket detector machine I described in the last chapter. We showed the children complicated patterns of contingency between the blocks and the detector. The children were like scientists looking at a big data table about smoking levels and cancer rates. Instead of asking what causes cancer or how to stop it, we asked similar questions about our machine. We asked the children which blocks made the machine go, and we also asked them to get it to stop.

For example, we showed children the two patterns of blocks in the figure below. In both cases, the white block makes the detector go three times and the black block makes it go two out of three times. If children were just looking at how often the blocks made the detector go they should behave the same way in both experiments. But the pattern of probabilities is different: black makes the detector go only if white is there too. You have to "factor out"

Screening-off Procedure

ONE-CAUSE CONDITION

| Object A activates the detector by itself. | Object B does not activate the detector by itself. | Both objects activate the detector (demonstrated twice). | Children are asked if each one is a blicket. |

TWO-CAUSE CONDITION

| Object A activates the detector by itself (demonstrated three times). | Object B does not activate the detector by itself (demonstrated once). | Object B activates the detector by itself (demonstrated twice). | Children are asked if each one is a blicket. |

Figure 1. The "Is It a Blicket?" experiment.
Source: Gopnik, Sobel, Schulz, and Glymour, 2001

the white block, the way we factor out age or income when we explore the link between smoking and cancer.

Three- and four-year-olds, and even two-year-olds, get it right. They say that the white block is a blicket but the black one is not in the first "one-cause" case, but that they both are blickets in the second "two-cause" condition. They make the sort of statistical inferences a scientist would make in order to find out the truth about the machine.

What is more, children can use their new knowledge about blickets to make changes, though admittedly rather small ones, in the world around them. For example, we can show children the sequence of events in the next picture. The black block goes on and nothing happens. Then we take it off and put the white block on by itself. The detector lights up and plays music. Now we add the black block to the top of the detector and the box still lights up and plays music. So both blocks are on top of the box and the box is playing. Then we ask the children to make the machine stop. Children have never actually seen anything make the machine stop, but nevertheless they make the right decision: Taking the white block off will work and taking the black block off won't. In a small way, the children in these experiments have learned how to change the world. In the "two-cause" condition, on the other hand, children figure out that they must take off both blocks.

We can even show that these young children are unconsciously calculating probabilities. We showed the children one block that made the detector go two out of six times and another that made it go two out of four times. Four-year-olds, who can't yet do simple addition, said that the second block had more of an effect on the detector than the first one. And in other experiments we showed that they used even more sophisticated Bayesian reasoning to calculate the probability of causes and effects.

Procedure used in Gopnik et al. (2001), Experiment 3

ONE-CAUSE CONDITION

Object B is placed on the detector and nothing happens.	Object B is removed.	Object A is placed on the detector by itself and the detector activates.	Object B is added to the detector with Object A. The detector continues to activate. Children are asked to make it stop.

TWO-CAUSE CONDITION

Object B is placed on the detector and the detector activates.	Object B is removed. The detector stops activating.	Object A is placed on the detector by itself and the detector activates.	Object B is added to the detector with Object A. The detector continues to activate. Children are asked to make it stop.

Figure 2. The "Make It Stop" experiment.
Source: Gopnik, Sobel, Schulz, and Glymour, 2001

EXPERIMENTATION: MAKING THINGS HAPPEN

In addition to making observations, scientists also learn about the causal structure of the world by performing experiments. In an experiment, the scientist intentionally acts on the world, she intervenes, just as she does when she uses her knowledge of the world to change it. But in an experiment the goal isn't to make something happen, it's to figure out *how* things happen. The scientist deliberately brings about a new event. She adds sulfuric acid to the sodium, or puts penicillin in the Petri dish of bacteria, and then observes what happens to the rest of the world, what other events follow. She can use this information to draw conclusions about the causal links between sodium and sulfuric acid or penicillin and bacteria out in the real world, even when she isn't intervening. Armed with these conclusions she can then go on to effectively change the world in a big way. She can cure tuberculosis and cholera by prescribing penicillin, for example.

When we just observe two events co-occur, it could always be because there's some hidden common cause we don't know about—maybe everyday stress makes people have high blood pressure and it also makes them get heart diseases. But now suppose we take a group of people and randomly give half of them a drug that lowers their blood pressure. If they get less heart disease, it must be because of the drug. Mathematically speaking, we can use Bayes-net models to show that these inferences about causation are justified by particular patterns of experimental results. Mathematicians can also show why experimentation is a particularly powerful way of learning about causes, providing much more accurate results than observation alone. And this work shows that you don't have to do the kinds of formal experiments that scientists perform to learn about causes. Other kinds of interventions that look more like children's play can also help us learn.

Can babies do experiments? Even very young babies pay special attention to the consequences of their actions. For example, we can attach a mobile to a three-month-old baby's leg with a ribbon, so that the baby's kicking makes the mobile move, and the baby will kick like mad. Is this a kind of experiment or is it just that the baby likes to see things move? To test this, you can show the same baby a mobile that does exactly the same things but isn't connected to the baby's own body. Babies prefer to look at the mobile that they can influence themselves, and they smile and coo at it more too. This suggests that it isn't just that they like the effect—they really are trying to make the effect happen and to see the consequences. They are happy because the experiment succeeds.

Moreover, babies will systematically explore the contingencies between various limb movements and the movements of the mobile—they'll try kicking with one leg and then another and then try waving an arm, watching the mobile's responses all the time. And if you take them out of the crib and then put them back in again they'll immediately wave the correct leg to make the mobile move. These explorations really do seem to be experiments. They are actions designed to find out about how the world works, rather than just actions designed to bring about particular events.

These very early experiments seem designed to find out about the direct causal links between what a baby does and what happens next. But by the time they are a year old babies will systematically vary the actions they perform on objects. Piaget described this kind of experimental play long ago. Rather than just doing the same thing over and over, say banging the block on the table, babies will first bang the block harder and then softer or first bang it and then shake it, carefully observing what happens all the while. And they don't just watch the immediate consequences of their actions; they watch the further consequences "downstream." Give an eighteen-month-old a set of blocks and you can see her trying different combinations, placements, and angles, seeing which ones eventually lead to stable towers and which end in an equally satisfying crash.

By the time children are four they do more complex experiments. Consider another demonic machine Laura Schulz and I designed—the gear toy. Like the blicket detector, the gear toy presents children with a new causal problem. It's a square box with two gears on top and a switch on the side. When you flip the switch the gears turn simultaneously. By itself that doesn't tell you how the toy works. But if you take off gear A and flip the switch, gear B turns by itself; if you take off gear B and flip the switch, gear A doesn't turn. With both these experiments together, you can conclude that the switch is making gear B move and that gear B is making gear A move.

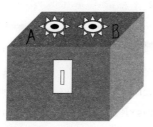

Figure 3. The gear toy.

If you feel a little shaky about following this, don't worry, you're in good company. When we did similar experiments with UC Berkeley undergraduates they got flummoxed when they tried to think it through. They did much better when we told them to just follow their instincts.

(My deception of my poor son Andres over the blicket detector came back to bite me with the gear toy. As psychologists, and thus mechanical incompetents, we asked the guys in the machine shop to make the toy for us. Several months later the machine broke and we asked them to replace the wires between the switches and the gears. They explained that actually there was no causal relationship between the gears and the switch at all. They had designed it so that each component had an independent microchip that made it act the right way—their version of the little man behind the curtain. This time I was the one who felt like Neo in *The Matrix*.)

We told four-year-olds to figure out how the toy worked and we left them alone and filmed them with a hidden camera. The children, just as you'd expect, played with the machine. They spun the gears around, listened to the inside of the box, even sniffed the machine. But they also kept flicking the switch, taking off gears and putting them on again. In the course of merely play-ing around, most of the children solved the problem.

Laura Schulz then provided even more striking evidence that young children use play experimentally to figure out causal prob-lems. She showed four-year-olds a box with two levers. In one ver-sion the experimenter said, "Here's your lever and my lever. Let's find out what these levers do," and pushed on her own lever simul-taneously with the child. A duck popped out of the box. This meant that the children didn't know which lever caused the duck to appear—it could have been either one. The other version was exactly the same except that this time the child and the experi-menter pushed the levers separately and the duck appeared only when one of the levers was pressed—it was obvious that that lever made the duck appear. Then Schulz simply left the children with the box. They played with the box much more in the first version than in the more obvious second one, pressing and manipulating the levers until they figured out just how the box worked.

In another experiment Christine Legare took our blicket de-tector and added in a small twist. One group of preschool children saw that blocks made the box go. But another group saw that three blocks worked, but then saw that one block didn't work. Christine asked the children, "Why did that happen?" and then she let them play with the box. Children gave a bunch of interesting explana-tions: "You put it in the wrong place!" or "The battery's dead!" or "It just looks like a blicket, it isn't one really." The children who saw the puzzling event played with the box much longer than the chil-dren who saw the regular box. And they played in a way that re-flected their explanations—the kids who said the last block wasn't really a blicket carefully made a pile of the good blickets and seg-regated them from the defective one.

This won't surprise anyone who has spent much time with babies or young children. We take it for granted that young children are perpetually "getting into things." In fact, a major job for caregivers is to keep this instinct for getting into such things as plugs and electric fans from causing harm. As a do-it-yourself exercise in developmental psychology, find any child between one and two, and simply watch her play with her toys for half an hour. Then count up the number of experiments you see—any child will put the most productive scientist to shame.

But when you think about it more closely this is a very odd thing for children to do. They don't get into things in order to satisfy their immediate needs; their immediate needs are taken care of by adults. Why do young children expend so much energy and time, even putting their own safety at risk? It makes perfect sense, though, if you think of toddlers as causal learning machines. Experimentation is one of the best ways of discovering new causes and their effects and understanding the causes you've already observed. The Mars rovers, perhaps the most dramatic recent discovery machines, get into everything too.

Although preschool teachers and parents have long felt intuitively that play contributes to learning, these experiments actually show scientifically that this is true. Just as imaginative play helps children explore possibilities, exploratory play lets them learn about the world. You can only hope that this will slow down the Dickensian administrators who seem to want to take play out of the early curriculum.

The drive to experiment seems to be innate, but experimentation provides us with a way of learning things that are not innate. What are built in are techniques for discovering all the things that aren't built in. Experimentation, in children or in scientists, provides us with a continuous series of shocks, little unexpected confrontations with nature. It's the key to solving Plato's problem. When we actively experiment on the world, we are really and truly interacting with a real world outside ourselves, and we can't tell beforehand what lessons that real world will teach.

DEMONSTRATION: WATCHING MOM'S EXPERIMENTS

Finally, there is a causal learning technique that lies somewhere between statistical analysis and active experimentation. It may be the most important kind of learning for us humans. Scientists learn from other people's experiments as well as their own. In fact, much scientific practice, from reading journals to going to talks, to holding lab meetings, helps you learn from other people. We scientists make the assumption that the interventions of others are like our own interventions and that we can learn the same things from both sources. By now each issue of a journal such as *Science* reflects the accumulated experiments of tens of thousands of scientists.

Learning from the actions of others was a basic mechanism of human culture long before organized science. By watching what others do and learning from it, we can go beyond the brief scope of an individual life. We can benefit from the accumulated learning of all the generations before us.

Experimental interventions are a particularly powerful way of learning about the causal structure of the world, much more powerful than mere observation alone, but there is a tension between the two kinds of learning. We can draw much stronger conclusions from experimentation than from observation, but it is much easier to observe than it is to experiment. Experimenting means acting and acting takes energy and resources and determination. However, if you assumed that other people's actions were similar to yours, you could vastly extend the scope of your experience with little expenditure of effort yourself. You could let other people do your experiments for you.

If those other people already knew more than you did, you could get special benefits from watching their interventions. Like the lab demonstrations in a science class, the interventions of "experts" can teach you what causes what.

Babies are particularly well designed to learn from other people in this way. They already know that other people intervene in the world the same way that they do. Seven-month-olds, for example, appreciate that actions are directed toward particular goals. To show this, Amanda Woodward used the habituation technique. You can show the babies two toys, say, a ball and a teddy bear on a table (see figure 4). A hand reaches in and grasps the teddy bear. Now you switch the locations of the two toys, so that the teddy bear is where the ball was and vice versa. What will the baby predict will happen next? Will the person they're watching move to the other side of the table to get the teddy bear? Or will she just go to the same side of the table as before? Seven-month-olds seem to predict that she'll reach for the teddy bear— they look longer when she goes to the ball instead. Even more strikingly, they don't make this prediction if a stick, rather than

a. Habituation   b. New Goal   c. Old Goal

Figure 4. The Woodward "Understanding Goals" experiment.
Source: Courtesy of Amanda Woodward

a hand, touches one object or the other. So seven-month-olds know that Mom's hands, like their own hands, try to make things happen.

Other kinds of experiments also show that a baby can link her own actions and the actions of others. For example, very young babies can imitate the actions of others—they will reproduce the actions they see someone else perform. Andy Meltzoff is the king of imitation research. Back in the seventies he showed that literally from the time they are born babies imitate the gestures and actions of other people. Nine-month-old babies can use this kind of imitation to learn about causes. These babies don't just imitate actions, they recognize and reproduce the results of those actions. For example, a one-year-old walks into the lab and sees the experimenter tap his head on a box, which makes it light up. A week later she returns to the lab and sees the box on the table. She'll immediately use her own head to get the box to light up.

By the time they are eighteen months old babies can imitate in an even more sophisticated way. Gyorgy Gergeley showed babies an experimenter touching her head to the box, but now she had a blanket wrapped around her so that her hands weren't available. If the other person's hands are free the babies will tap their own heads on the machine. But if she's wrapped up in the blanket and she taps the machine with her head, the babies will instead use their own hands. They seem to have figured out that you would use your hands if you could, but since you can't you're using your head instead.

Or suppose you show the baby someone trying to take apart a two-part toy dumbbell, as Meltzoff did. The baby sees the other person try and try again, but never manage actually to succeed. When they get the toy the babies immediately pull apart the toy themselves. As all parents wryly recognize, children don't just learn by imitating your successes. They learn by avoiding your mistakes, and understanding your limitations, too.

These babies go beyond simply imitating the other person. Instead they recognize the complex causal relationships among human goals, actions, and outcomes.

By the time they're four, children can use information about your interventions to make very complicated new causal inferences. For example, take the "gear toy" experiment I described before. The children experimented on the toy until they saw the right pattern of evidence to figure out how the toy worked. But instead of trying out all the different possibilities themselves, they could just watch what another person did to make the toy go. It turns out that children will also solve this problem if they simply see an adult demonstrate the right experiments on the toy, as well as when they perform the experiments themselves.

This suggests that other people, especially caregivers, can serve as implicit causal tutors for children—long before children have any formal education. When adults demonstrate actions, and encourage babies and children to imitate them, they also encourage causal learning. They demonstrate the particular tricks and tools of their individual culture, but they also point to the causal relations that those tricks and tools exploit.

In fact, for most of human history, this kind of demonstration was the most significant educational technique. In preindustrial societies it still is. Barbara Rogoff studied Mayan mothers and children in Guatemala. She found that the Mayan children developed a remarkable degree of skill with complex and dangerous tools at a very early age. Young children are constantly with the adults as the adults practice these skills—the village square is both the workplace and the childcare center—and adults make sure that even the youngest babies carefully watch what they do.

This kind of demonstration also provides a powerful mechanism for change and innovation. A single new discovery by a clever, or lucky, experimenter can spread through an entire community and on to the next generation, until it seems second nature to the generation that learned it as small children. Each culture can develop its own special expertise this way. Barbara Rogoff told me that, on a trip to the city, the Mayan mothers marveled at the way Barbara's own children effortlessly coped with the complexities of a bathroom, manipulating all those complicated levers and taps with hardly a second thought. The Mayan mothers had the same astonished reaction that Barbara did when she saw the Mayan children skillfully manage machetes and cooking fires.

You can learn a causal map by watching the consequences of particular actions—by seeing how a number of experiments turned out. But once you've learned the map you can do much more than just reproduce the actions you've seen. Causal maps also let you consider new possibilities and make new plans. The children who watched us manipulate the gear toy could figure out new ways to make it go or stop. Watching an expert demonstrate how to use a machete doesn't just let you perform the same moves that the expert does. It also lets you understand how machetes work, and so lets you think of new ways to use the machete to solve new problems.

UNDERSTANDING MINDS

So far, I've talked about how babies learn about physical causes—gears and switches, blickets and blicket detectors. But for human beings psychological causes are just as important—maybe more so. We saw earlier that just as babies and children learn a great deal about physical causes they also learn a great deal about psychological causes. Even the youngest babies already seem to understand some basic facts about emotion and action. But as they grow older they gradually develop an understanding of desire, perception, and belief, personality traits, moods, and prejudices, all the way up to the detailed and subtle psychology we can appreciate in Lady Murasaki or Proust. But though we've shown *that* children learn about other minds, we haven't yet explained *how* they learn.

Children learn about physical and psychological causes in similar ways. At first it might seem that there's not much connection between the statistical analyses that let us discover that smoking causes lung cancer, or even that the blickets make the detector go, and everyday psychology. But, in fact, statistical patterns may actually help us to identify which things have minds in the first place.

Think about the ways we interact with people and with things. When we manipulate things, typically it's all or nothing. When I pick up a ball it follows my every move. When I put it down it doesn't do a thing. The same with light switches and remote controls. But with people it's all much more complex and delicate. Sometimes when you smile at Mom she smiles back, but sometimes she's distracted or busy. And if you do smile at Mom and she smiles back that will make you more likely to smile, which will make her more likely to smile, and so on. Sometimes we interact with a physical object that has the same pattern of complex responses as a person. My computer, for instance, mostly does what I tell it to do, but sometimes it's practically perverse, refusing to perform no matter what I do, or worse, behaving itself one minute and then seizing up the next. In those cases we often feel as if the computer has a mind of its own.

Even one-year-olds are sensitive to these contingency patterns, and use them to differentiate people and things. The psychologist Susan Johnson endowed a very clearly nonhuman thing, a sort of brown robotic blob, with the ability to react contingently to a baby. When the baby made a noise, the blob chirped, and when the baby moved, the blob lit up, and so forth. A second identical blob made the same chirps and lit up the same way but did so in a way that was entirely unrelated to what the baby did. The events were the same, but the statistical relations between the events were different—the chirps were correlated with the babies' actions in one case but not the other.

Then each blob turned so that one end of it faced away from the baby and toward an object. The babies turned to follow the "gaze" of the reactive blob but not the unreactive blob. They seemed to think that the reactive blob could see. And the babies babbled and gestured more at the blob that interacted with them than at the blob that didn't.

They also treated the reactive blob as if it had goals. They seemed to think that it wanted things. Remember that babies understood that someone was trying to pull apart a toy dumbbell even when they didn't manage to succeed. They didn't react the same way to a machine. But when Johnson gave the machine interactive abilities, when it chirped and lit up in response, then the babies did act as if the machine was trying to pull apart the toy. In short, they treated a reactive object, even a very peculiar reactive object, as if it had a mind, and as if the pattern of its chirps and lights and movements were indications of what it saw and wanted to do.

We can also do psychological versions of exactly the same experiments we did with the blicket detector. By the time they're four years old children will use statistical patterns to make inferences about individual minds. This time, instead of showing children blocks and machines, we showed them a toy bunny in a basket. The bunny, we told them, is scared of some animals but not others, and we wanted them to figure out the bunny's fears. Then children saw various patterns of contingency relating the bunny and other toy animals. A zebra showed up in the basket by itself and the bunny shook with fright. But when an elephant appeared by himself, the bunny welcomed him in. Then the elephant and the zebra both appeared in the bunny's basket and the bunny shook with fright again. Could the children "factor out" the effects of the elephant, and conclude that the bunny was really scared only of the zebra?

Four-year-olds drew the right conclusions about what made the bunny scared—they analyzed the data and figured out the right answer. They could also intervene in the world to change it based on this knowledge—they would remove the zebra from the basket to ensure the bunny's peace of mind (and indeed the sympathetic preschoolers were quite anxious to do so—they practically rushed in to evict the scary animal from the basket even before we asked them to).

Children can draw conclusions about personality traits in the same way. My student Elizabeth Seiver and I showed four-year-olds different patterns of contingency among people, situations, and actions. Anna and Josie were little dolls that could play on a miniature trampoline and bicycle. We showed half the children that Anna happily went on the trampoline and leaped on the bicycle three out of four times but Josie could bring herself to get on the trampoline and bicycle only one out of four times. We showed the other half of the children that Anna and Josie both happily bounced on the trampoline three out of four times but dared approach the bicycle only one out of four times. Again the events were the same but the statistical patterns were different.

Then we asked the children to explain why Anna and Josie acted the way they did. The first group said it was because Anna was brave and Josie was timid, and they predicted that Anna would continue to be brave in new situations—she'd go off the diving board, too. The second group said the dolls acted that way because the trampoline was safe and the bicycle was dangerous. Watching the pattern of playground behavior can lead children to some deep conclusions about what other people are like.

Often these inferences are right, of course, but even very young children, like adults, may make profound decisions about someone's character with just a little data. You may be quick to decide that a colleague is a really good guy when he smiles at you a few times (and then be startled to discover what he's really like). Sometimes this can even be a matter of life and death. People in general concluded that the abusive Abu Ghraib guards had deep-seated evil personality traits, even though psychological research suggests that many, even most people, might act similarly in those situations.

Children learn from the patterns they see, but they also perform psychological experiments to explore the inner as well as the outer world. For example, Ed Tronick got nine-month-olds to watch their mothers suddenly adopt a perfectly still pose—a kind of impassive, iron face. As you might expect, the babies were perturbed by this, and often even started crying. But they would also produce a large number of unusual and expressive gestures, as if they were trying somehow to test what was wrong. In another study, instead of having a baby imitate an adult, the adult imitated the baby, mimicking everything that the baby did. Faced with this extremely peculiar behavior, one-year-olds performed a different kind of experiment. They produced odd exaggerated gestures as if they were testing whether the experimenter really would imitate those actions too. They would wiggle a hand in some particularly strange way to see if the adult would do the same. The babies were as intrigued by the mimicry as they were by the stone face and, in each case, they tried to get a reaction from the adult that would help them figure out what was going on.

Perhaps most potent of all, children can learn about the mind by observing the interactions and interventions of people around them. Watching how the people around you influence and manipulate others is a particularly powerful source of information about psychological causes. Younger siblings, for example, rather surprisingly seem to learn about minds more quickly than older siblings, though they typically do worse on IQ and verbal tests. Younger siblings develop exceptional emotional and social intelligence, while older ones develop more conventional schoolroom intelligence. Younger siblings are more likely to be peacemakers and charmers, while older siblings are the serious achievers. Watching an older brother or sister interact with Mom and Dad may be a very important way of learning how minds work. Younger siblings have especially rich opportunities to see Machiavellian intelligence in action. When he was two, my middle son would stare from his high chair with utter fascination at his three-year-old brother—noting every argument lost and won, every negotiation, every little bit of three-year-old diplomacy and strategy.

Language plays an especially potent role in learning about the mind. In fact, there are consistent and strong correlations between children's language abilities and their understanding of the minds of others. After all, a major way that we come to understand what is going on in other people's heads is by hearing what they say. We can figure out how objects work by looking at them and we can even figure out what people want by looking at what they do. But to figure out what people think, you have to hear what they say.

Perhaps the most dramatic example of the power of language comes from deaf children. Deaf children of deaf parents, who learn sign as a native language and are surrounded by other signers, have no trouble understanding minds. However, most deaf children have hearing parents. Even when those parents learn sign, as most do nowadays, they use it rather haltingly as a second language, the way I would speak Spanish if I suddenly tried to learn it now. As a result deaf children of hearing parents often don't understand what the people around them are saying. This means they miss much of the psychological interaction that is going on around them. They also have a particularly hard time understanding minds. Remember that five-year-olds, unlike three-year-olds, usually understand that beliefs can be false—they say that Nick will think there are candies in the candy box, even though really it's full of pencils. But deaf children of hearing parents who don't use sign may not solve this problem until they are eight or nine.

Even more dramatically, studying deaf children lets us see what happens when a language is actually created. In Nicaragua, as in many poor and small countries, deaf children were traditionally isolated from one another—they didn't have a common language and no one taught them sign language. In the seventies, for the first time, Nicaragua opened a school for the deaf, where all the children could meet one another and communicate. The children actually started to invent a new sign language. By the time the next generation of children arrived they could learn this new language instead of trying to cobble it together themselves. It was a natural experiment on the benefits of language.

Jennie Pyers went to study these children. She discovered that the first generation of children—the ones who had to invent the language—had a terrible time understanding how other people's minds worked, like other deaf children of hearing parents. You could see this in laboratory tests but you could also see it in their everyday lives. Even adults couldn't solve the simple problem about the pencils in the candy box. If you asked them to describe a video of a man absentmindedly taking a teddy bear from a hat rack and putting it on his head instead of a hat, they never mentioned that maybe he had made a mistake. The other deaf people at the school commented on how hapless their older friends were at keeping secrets or manipulating other people. The second generation of children, who had all learned a common language, had no trouble understanding how minds worked. Even though they were younger than the previous generation they had no trouble solving the candies-and-pencils problem. They immediately said that the man in the video must have thought the bear was his hat.

In fact, psychology is an arena where the premodern ways of teaching are still the most effective ones, even in contemporary life. We don't teach psychology in elementary schools, because we don't need to. Every distracted or commanding teacher, every successful bully or heroic defier of bullying, every charming flirt or captivating class clown, is a rich psychology tutorial of their own.

While a new tool or technique, a wheel or a lever, may be impressive, the psychological wheels and levers are really the things that move the world. Mastering physical causality can give us the means to explore space or destroy the world. But psychological causality, the words spoken by some humans to others, actually makes the rockets go up or the bombs come down.

Our ability to represent the causal structure of the world and the mind and to imagine and create possible new worlds and minds is one powerful engine of human change. But our ability to revise and transform those representations, to observe and experiment, and to learn from those observations and experiments gives us an even more powerful engine of change. A single accurate causal map already allows us to change the world in myriad ways. But the ability to create new and ever more accurate causal maps, both of the world and ourselves, lets us do even more.

This ability to learn about the causal structure of the world may lie at the heart of what makes us distinctively human. The two most prominent theories of the evolution of human intelligence both emphasize causal knowledge. One school emphasizes the importance of understanding physical causes—the sort of understanding that allowed us to use complex tools. Another emphasizes the ability to understand psychological causes—the sort of understanding that allowed us to maintain complex social networks and to develop culture.

Our ability to learn about causes may underlie both these valuable and distinctively human abilities. We should, of course, be wary of saying that there are things that only humans can do. Many animals are better at using tools and understanding the actions of other animals than we once thought. And we should avoid the hubris of thinking that these capacities are somehow "higher" or "more evolved" than others. We have been around for only about one-hundredth as long as the dinosaurs, and our capacities for tool use and complex social networks may yet lead to our extinction.

However, even if other animals have some of these capacities, we are, at the very least, much better at these kinds of learning than any other animal, and we devote far more of our time and energy to their pursuit. And we do this most of all when we are very small children.

Thinking about Plato's problem—how we learn—can help us understand many otherwise puzzling facts about children, such as their obsessive, tireless experimental play and their ceaseless observation and imitation of adults. Why does my one-year-old get into everything? Why does my two-year-old always press my buttons? Where on earth did my three-year-old get *that* from? Children act this way just because they are designed to rapidly and accurately learn the causal structure of the physical and psychological worlds around them.

At the same time, the discovery that even the youngest children are so deeply engaged in causal learning, and are so good at it too, suggests a new way of thinking about the ancient philosophical questions. Plato and other philosophers asked, "How can we know so much about the world?" The scientific answer is that methods of experimentation and statistical analysis seem to be programmed into our brains even when we are tiny babies. Very young children unconsciously use these techniques to change their causal maps of the world. Those programs allow babies, and so the rest of us, to find the truth.

4.

What Is It Like to Be a Baby?

CONSCIOUSNESS AND ATTENTION

*

The great developmental psychologist John Flavell once told me that he would trade all his degrees and honors for the chance to spend just five minutes inside the head of a young child—to genuinely experience the world as a two-year-old once more. I think this is the secret wish of almost all developmental psychologists however scientifically we may talk about neural plasticity and fundamental learning mechanisms. And it occurs to every parent, too. What is it like to be a baby? How do babies experience the world? What does knowing about consciousness tell us about babies and young children? What can babies and young children tell us about the nature of consciousness?

At least since the scientific revolution began, consciousness has been one of the thorniest problems in philosophy. All of us know that we have specific vivid experiences—the special tint of a blue-grey sky, the distinctive taste of ripe strawberries, the particular pitch of a pigeon's coo. Philosophers invent technical terms to capture this special quality of our experience like "subjectivity" or "qualia." But perhaps the best philosophical expression of the problem comes from Thomas Nagel. In a famous essay Nagel asked, "What is it like to be a bat?" The problem of consciousness is about what it is like to be me.

Before we knew much about the brain it was possible to see consciousness as a mysterious feature of a special kind of substance—whether you call it mind or soul. But a hundred years or more of scientific study of the brain has convinced almost all philosophers that everything we experience must be connected to, or caused by, or based in the brain (the very profusion of prepositions is revealing). Still, though, the problem of how that is possible is not much nearer a solution than it was one hundred years ago. How can the electrical activity of a few pounds of grey goo produce the blue of the sky and the song of the dove?

For most problems, including most philosophical problems, we can at least get a hint of what the possible solutions might be. The problem is to decide which solution is the right one. But consciousness is one of those really tough, frustrating problems where we don't have a clue about what the solutions should even look like. The one thing that seems clear is that the possibilities on offer are all pretty hopeless.

Usually in cognitive science we explain how the mind works by thinking about the actions we produce or the computations we perform. We explain the fact that we can produce new sentences by saying that we know linguistic rules. If we had different rules we would produce different types of sentences. However, consciousness doesn't seem to be just the result of having a brain that produces certain behaviors or performs particular computations. At least it seems as if we might have just the same rules and produce just the same kinds of sentences, and yet experience language completely differently. It even seems possible that robots could produce those behaviors or perform those computations without any awareness at all. Consciousness also seems to be more than just the result of having particular kinds of neural connections, or a particular evolutionary history. We can at least imagine zombies who were like us in every respect but had no awareness.

Another possibility, dualism, the idea that there is some separate spooky substance responsible for consciousness, just doesn't fit with everything else we know about science—even when it's dolled up in talk about quantum mechanics. This hasn't stopped philosophers from arguing for all these options and more, but I think at heart even the most fervent advocates feel unsatisfied with the answers.

There are two rays of hope in this otherwise dismal picture. First, we've been here before. For centuries, the problem of life loomed as large and seemed as intractable as the problem of consciousness does now. How could all the special properties of living things come from a collection of atoms and molecules that aren't alive at all? The answer turned out to be that the question was wrong—instead of a single explanation of "life" we have lots of little explanations about how particular configurations of molecules could lead to particular properties of living things.

This example may be particularly relevant because of the other ray of hope. While we don't know how "Capital C" Consciousness is related to the brain, we know an increasing amount about how particular features of consciousness are related to particular psychological and neural states. We actually know quite a lot, for example, about why green seems to be composed of yellow and blue, why the moon appears larger when it's near the horizon, why the rest of the world disappears when we are absorbed in work, and so on.

Much of what we've learned about consciousness is counterintuitive. For example, consider "blindsight." Certain patients with brain damage have no conscious visual experience at all; they swear up and down that they are blind in part of their visual field. But if you insist that they just make a wild guess—"You don't understand," they protest, "I can't *see*"—they can figure out where objects are and even what shape they are. They will reach accurately for a ball they can't see. Recently, scientists showed that you could get just the same effect in ordinary people by temporarily inactivating their visual cortex.

Even in everyday life sight is more complicated than it seems. It turns out that we don't actually get any visual input at a central spot near the back of the eye; it's called the blind spot. If a light shines at that particular spot on your retina you won't see anything. But, of course, we don't experience that hole at all. We "fill in" so that it seems we have a smooth, unbroken visual field. Surely we should know what we see, but does the person with blindsight really see the ball? Do we see the blind spot?

Looking at the way babies and young children experience the world can provide us with equally counterintuitive insights about consciousness. Just as the experience of blindsight patients may ultimately give us cues about consciousness, so we can hope that understanding children's experience will ultimately help us understand how consciousness can exist at all.

How can we tell what it's like to be a baby? Babies and young children can't tell us about their experiences. None of us accurately remembers our infancy, and even our memories of early childhood are very hazy and unreliable. Nevertheless, it's possible to at least make an educated guess about what infant experience is like. We can use our knowledge about the psychological and neurological bases of adult experience, and our additional knowledge about the psychological and neurological differences between adults and children.

As adults, we become vividly aware of objects when we pay attention to them. When we pay attention to objects our brains produce neurotransmitters that make certain neurons work better and change more easily. Babies pay attention in systematically different ways than adults, and their brains work differently too. These differences suggest that baby consciousness may be systematically different from that of adults.

This leads to a counterintuitive but fascinating conclusion. Many philosophers have suggested that babies are somehow less conscious than adults are, if they are conscious at all. After all, babies don't have the ability to talk or to explicitly reason their way through a problem or to make complex plans, abilities that are related to consciousness for adults. The philosopher Peter Singer has even notoriously argued on this basis that disabled infants have no more intrinsic right to live than nonhuman animals do—for Singer we have as much justification to kill babies as to kill other animals for meat. Whatever you think of Singer's ethical claim, or about animal consciousness, I think his factual claim is just wrong. The data lead to just the opposite conclusion—babies are, at least by some measures, *more* conscious than we are.

EXTERNAL ATTENTION

Attention and consciousness seem to be closely related. When I attend to something carefully I become vividly conscious of it. Many psychologists use the metaphor of a spotlight to describe these effects of attention—when we attend to something it's as if we shine a beam of light on it that makes all its details brighter and more vivid.

Sometimes we pay attention because an external object catches our eye—a big truck suddenly looms in front of us. Psychologists call this exogenous attention. But we can also voluntarily shift our attention, and our consciousness, from one object to another— endogenous attention. We can say to ourselves, "This is a dangerous corner. Pay attention!" and the traffic suddenly comes into clear and vivid focus.

New or unexpected events are especially likely to catch our attention. Some kinds of events, like loud noises, may just be intrinsically startling. But we also pay attention to more subtly unexpected events. When you live near a railway and become used to the trains you may wake up startled when a train doesn't go by at the usual time. When we experience something new, or startling, or salient, our brains produce characteristic electrical patterns— brain waves—that are associated with attention. As we try to make sense of the new event our bodies change as well as our minds— our heart rate slows in a distinctive way—and we enter an especially vivid state of consciousness.

You can do an experiment that is the equivalent of the train that doesn't go by. You play a certain pattern of sounds repeatedly, and then fail to play a sound at the accustomed time. Although nothing has actually happened, your brain responds as if it had heard a startling new sound. Paradoxically, we may actually become more aware of the deafening silence than we were of the sound. (In a good suspense movie the moments of expectation when nothing actually happens are often far more vivid than all the explosions and shoot-outs.)

Just as an unexpected silence can be deafening, an expected noise can become silent. After a while, as we take in all the information we can, we become used to the sound, "habituated" like the babies in the looking and listening experiments I described earlier. We get bored, and both our attention and our vivid consciousness trail off. When we become completely habituated to an event our consciousness of it may disappear almost entirely. We may literally no longer hear the train that goes by each day at noon. When we first move into a new house we are aware of every detail of each new room, but after a few months the place can become practically invisible.

Similarly, when we first master a new skill, such as riding a bike or using a new computer program, we are painfully conscious of every step. But by the time we become expert we can literally be completely unconscious of what we are doing. We know so much about the house or bicycle riding or the computer program, and what we know is so well learned, that we no longer need to pay attention. We no longer need to take in any additional information or learn anything new about the event or skill—we just do it. In adult life it sometimes feels as if hours and even days can go by when we are on autopilot this way—perfectly functional, walking, talking, teaching, meeting-attending zombies.

INTERNAL ATTENTION

For adults, attention can also be endogenous, directed voluntarily at particular objects, like that spotlight. In this case, attending to one thing can actually make us much less conscious of the other things around us, even salient or new or unexpected things. When I'm walking down the street absorbed in a problem I'm notoriously likely to bump into the lamppost that would otherwise be perfectly apparent—a living cliché of the absentminded professor, as my children often point out.

There are some startling experimental demonstrations of this effect. Some psychologists call it "inattentional blindness." In one dramatic experiment, designed by Dan Simons, you look at a video of several people throwing a ball. The instruction is to count the number of times the ball goes from hand to hand. The players weave in and out so this takes some effort; it's like trying to follow the pea in the old shell game. Then the experimenter asks if you noticed anything strange. "Nothing," you say. Now he plays the video again, but this time he says you don't have to follow the ball. And you see that someone in a gorilla suit walked slowly right through the middle of the scene! You were looking right at the gorilla but literally didn't see it, because your attention was so focused on the ball. (I saw this video again recently at a meeting of the Association for the Scientific Study of Consciousness. The presenter first said, "All of you know this clip." And indeed all of us did except George Johnson, a science journalist for *The New York Times*, who was sitting beside me. George stared completely blank-faced, counting the balls, utterly oblivious as the gorilla walked through the scene and everyone laughed. At the end he turned to me, puzzled, and said, "What was the point of that? Why did they laugh?")

It turns out that there are neurological bases for these effects. When we attend to something our brain releases a particular kind of chemical, called a cholinergic transmitter. This chemical affects how well neurons function—it makes them conduct information better. The nicotine in cigarettes mimics these transmitters and literally makes you more attentive, just as opium mimics the natural transmitters that kill pain. When we pay attention our brains release these transmitters quite selectively, just to the particular parts of the brain that are processing information about the event we attend to. At the same time our brains also release inhibitory transmitters and activate inhibitory neurons that have just the opposite effect on other parts of the brain. (Coffee also makes us alert but it seems to do so by inhibiting some of these inhibitors—coffee opens up our attention and cigarettes let it narrow in on a particular target. It's no wonder they're the preferred drugs of journalists, who have to take in all the information about a breaking story and then summarize it in 250 words by a deadline.) What your brain actually does depends on the balance between the inhibitory effects and the excitatory ones. So paying attention literally boosts some parts of your brain and shuts down others.

Attention not only makes some parts of your brain work better, but it also makes those parts of your brain more plastic—that is, those parts of your brain change more easily than other parts of your brain. The evidence for this comes from studies of monkeys by Michael Merzenich and his colleagues. Neuroscientists can actually record the activity of a monkey's brain cells and see that different cells respond to different kinds of events. Some cells respond to particular kinds of sounds, for example, and others respond to touch.

The experimenters got the monkeys to pay attention to one type of event instead of another. A monkey hears a stream of sounds, say, and feels a sequence of touches. If he moves his hand when he hears a particular sound he gets some juice, but touch isn't rewarded. The monkey pays more attention to the sounds as a result, just as in a crowded room you might focus your attention on overhearing a potentially rewarding conversation and ignore the irrelevant ones.

When they checked the monkeys' brains they discovered that the sound cells had been rewired by these experiences—they responded differently—but the tactile cells were the same. In fact, more of the monkeys' brain cells responded to sound after they had been trained, but the number of touch-responding cells stayed the same. When they reversed the experiment so that touch was more rewarding, they got the reverse effect. These changes seem to be at least partly mediated by the cholinergic transmitters. If the monkeys were given a chemical that blocked those transmitters, the changes were less likely. This plasticity effect also seems to fit our intuition that when we attend to things carefully we can learn more about them than when we do not. When we learn we literally change our minds and brains in the light of new information.

Voluntary endogenous attention—as when I tell myself to pay attention to the traffic—is a way to persuade our brains to learn. It makes us treat something as if it were novel or unexpected, even when it isn't. As an adult I can simply decide that I need to get extra information in the service of some larger goal, like the monkey who pays attention to the sounds that will get him the juice. For example, I can force myself to follow the often mind-numbingly boring scientific papers on the neuropsychology of attention because I think the information will help me to be accurate when I'm writing my book. Given that goal, it's as important for me to attend to the papers as it is for me to take in information about some intrinsically attention-grabbing unexpected event—like the first scene of a Hitchcock movie. Or I can force myself to attend to the perfectly ordinary traffic at the busy corner because I know abstractly that something dangerous may happen.

So while we don't have a Big Explanation of Consciousness, we do have a story about how a particular kind of vivid, narrowly focused awareness is related to the mind and the brain. When we have this kind of consciousness our minds take in information about some parts of the world and shut out distracting information from others. And we can use the attended information to learn something new. Certain things also happen in our brains—they release cholinergic and inhibitory transmitters appropriately. In turn those transmitters both make the relevant parts of the brain function more efficiently and allow them to be reshaped more easily.

There is also a related story about a particular kind of unconsciousness. Many psychological and brain processes are simply never conscious at all. But in other cases, we actually make potentially conscious events become less conscious. When events or activities become familiar, well understood, and highly practiced they also become, as we say, automatic—less conscious than they were before. Similarly, when we focus our attention on one event we become less conscious of other unattended events. Inhibitory brain processes seem to be involved in both these kinds of unconsciousness.

BABY ATTENTION

What does all this have to do with babies? We don't know exactly what babies' conscious experience is like but we do know something about their capacity for attention and about their brains (or at least we know about the brains of baby monkeys and rats). Babies and young children are both similar to and different from adults in significant and revealing ways.

In the bad old days, psychologists thought that babies could attend only in an entirely automatic and reflexive way, without even using their higher brain centers at all. This was part of what I think of as the myth of the brain-deficient baby, the idea that newborn babies were crying carrots, vegetables with a few reflexes.

In fact, when babies attend to something they seem to take in information about it and to be conscious of it in the same way as adults. When they see even a subtly unexpected event they show the same brain waves that adults do. They look steadily and intently at the event, their eyes scan the important features of the event, and their heart rate decreases in the same way. Every sign

earlier mental states. We can see this in the "false belief" experiment I described before. Children see a closed candy box, which turns out to be full of pencils. The children are understandably both surprised and disappointed by this discovery. But then we asked what they thought was in the box when they first saw it. Although they had discovered the truth with great surprise only moments before, they still said that they had always known the box was full of pencils. They had entirely forgotten their earlier false belief.

We wondered if children forgot past desires as well as past beliefs. First, we asked children if they wanted crackers, and when they said yes we gave them crackers till they were positively stuffed, and refused to eat any more. Then we asked if they had wanted crackers when they first sat down, before they actually ate them. Half the three-year-olds said that they had never wanted the crackers at all. These children had no difficulty at all remembering past physical events, but they had a hard time remembering how they had felt about those events.

Trying to imagine what it is like to be a child in these experiments is as dislocating as trying to imagine what it is like to be H.M. You look at the tightly closed drawer and clearly hear me say there's an egg inside it, you are shocked to discover that there are pencils in the box, you are ravenous for the crackers. But literally minutes later you blithely, confidently, and sincerely remember that you saw the egg, believed that the box was full of pencils all along, and never wanted the crackers. It would seem that nothing could be more self-evident than our immediately past conscious experiences. And yet three-year-olds, who can remember specific events like moon watching for months, can't seem to recapture the experiences they had minutes before.

We adults may make these sorts of mistakes after a long time.

We may come to think that we always saw through communism, or that we actually attended the rally we only saw on TV, or that we couldn't possibly ever have liked Donovan. But children make these mistakes after just minutes have passed. They must be living in a very different world than we are.

CONSTRUCTING MYSELF

Autobiographical memory plays an important role in personal identity. I'm not continuous with my earlier and later selves because we share some particular characteristics—I am, after all, more like other fifty-year-old women developmental psychologists than I am like the three-year-old I was or the eighty-year-old that (with luck) I will be. And it isn't even because I maintain the same physical body over time—after all, my current body is (sadly) completely different from the body I had thirty years ago. The secret is memory. I can remember what I felt and thought and did earlier, even the now-strange thoughts and feelings of the six-year-old me (who believed that everyone in China lived in houses made of paper, and who was irrationally afraid of venturing into dark basements), or the even stranger thoughts and feelings of the sixteen-year-old me (who believed that everyone in China welcomed the Cultural Revolution, and who was irrationally unafraid of venturing into dark alleys).

Those memories are *mine*, and they are mine in a very distinctive and significant way. I may know about the equally strange thoughts and feelings that my brother once had, but I don't remember them and they aren't *my* past thoughts and feelings. In *Star Trek*, the most philosophically profound program ever to appear on television, there is a story that makes this point particularly clearly. Jadwiga Dax is a creature who consists of two parts, a regular body (Jadwiga) and a separate symbiont (Dax) that is transferred from one body to another as each body dies. Jadwiga takes on the accumulated knowledge of all the past lives of the symbiont, his skills at diplomacy and gambling, for example. But what actually makes Jadwiga and Dax a single person is that she also takes on the memories of all of Dax's previous lives, and experiences them in the same way that she experiences her own memories.

The philosopher John Campbell argues that the conscious experience of autobiographical memory depends on the causal relationship between our past selves and our current and future selves. As adults we think of our lives as a single unfolding causal story that links our past, present, and future experience. What we will do, feel, and believe in the future depends on what we do, feel, and believe now, which depends on what we did, felt, and believed in the past. This single timeline seems self-evident to us adults, but we could organize our experiences quite differently. People with dissociative or multiple-personality disorders, for example, have separate timelines for separate selves, so that what I do as Jekyll will influence Jekyll's future actions, but not my actions as Hyde.

Very young children already have some sense of self. For example, when they get to be around eighteen months old, children start to recognize themselves in the mirror. You can show this by surreptitiously putting a sticker on the baby's forehead and then putting her in front of a mirror. One-year-olds act as if there is another baby in the mirror and they point to the image of the sticker in the mirror. Two-year-olds, in contrast, immediately touch their own foreheads to see if the sticker is there.

But they don't seem to understand how this self is related to past and future selves—they don't have a single timeline. Teresa McCormack showed children two different series of pictures on two successive days. Then she asked the children which pictures they had seen, and whether they had seen them today or yesterday. The three-year-olds were very good at recognizing that they had seen the pictures but very bad at saying when they had seen them. By six years old children could do this about as well as adults.

Danny Povinelli did an even more dramatic experiment. Nowadays nearly all parents go around making videos of their preschoolers and playing them back, and even three-year-olds understand the basics of how videos work. In the experiment a grown-up played with a child and in the course of playing surreptitiously put a sticker on the child's forehead, just as in the experiment with the eighteen-month-old and the mirror. Immediately afterward he played a videotape of what had just happened back to the child. Five-year-olds were amazed to see the sticker in the videotape and immediately touched their foreheads to see if it was still there—they integrated the past self in the video and their current selves—but the three-year-olds were unfazed. They could recognize their present selves in a mirror, but they couldn't integrate the present and the past. Although they remarked that there was a sticker on their head in the video, they didn't seem to put that information about their past self together with their current self. They didn't seem to realize that having a sticker put on them five minutes ago meant that right now the sticker was still sitting on their forehead.

Tellingly, the three-year-olds also referred to the child on tape by using their own names, while the fours said that the child on the tape was "me." At three Johnny would say, "Look, Johnny has a sticker on his head," and make no attempt to touch his own head. At four he would say, "Look, I have a sticker on my head," and immediately reach to take it off. The younger children knew that the kid on the tape was them at an earlier time, but they didn't see the connection between the earlier Johnny and the person they were now.

All this has led many psychologists to argue that babies and young preschoolers don't have autobiographical memory in the same way that older children do or that we do. Memory researchers often treat episodic memory and autobiographical memory as two terms for the same thing—and, in fact, this seems to be true for adults. But you could say that babies and young children have episodic memory but not autobiographical memory. Although they are very good at remembering specific events in the past, they don't put these events into a single coherent timeline, don't remember how they know about the events, and don't remember their past attitudes toward events. They also don't privilege events that they have directly experienced over events they have learned about in other ways. And they don't have a single "inner autobiographer," a self who links their past and present mental states. They don't experience the "me" who used to think that there were pencils in the box, or who wanted the crackers before receiving the snack, or who had the sticker put on his head.

CHILDREN AND THE FUTURE

At the same time that four-year-olds begin to understand that their minds may have changed in the past, they also begin to understand that their minds may change in the future. In one experiment, Cristina Atance showed children pictures of different landscapes: a desert with a hot sun, or a snowy mountaintop. She said, "Suppose you were going to go for a trip here tomorrow. What should you take?" Children could choose between different objects: sunglasses or a seashell, a warm jacket or an ice cube.

Then she asked, "Why did you choose that?" Four- and five-year-olds chose the right option to protect against the perils of their imagined future (sunglasses for the desert, a warm jacket for the snow). They also explicitly explained those choices in terms of their anticipated future states: "In case my eyes hurt" or "I'm gonna get cold." But three-year-olds were much less likely to do this. They were as likely to think that you should take a seashell to the desert as sunglasses.

There is other evidence that babies and young children don't project themselves into the future in the same way that we do. At just about the same time that children are developing autobiographical memory they are also developing "executive control" abilities. Executive control is our ability to suppress what we want to do now because of what we will want in the future. We already saw that between three and five, children become able to act to change their own minds. They can sing or whistle or close their eyes to keep from trying to get that terribly tempting cookie.

We saw earlier that even young babies can make plans for the future. They can imagine an alternative way the world might be and act to make that alternative into reality. But executive control demands more than just making plans. I don't just have to imagine alternative ways the world might be, I have to imagine alternative ways that I might be. Usually when I make plans I do something to get what I want right now. Executive control becomes important when there is a conflict between what I want now and what I will want in the future. It requires me to understand the causal link between the way I feel now and the way I will feel later. Right now I don't need sunglasses and would love that one cookie. Afterward, when I get to the desert, or lose the two cookies, I'll feel differently. Executive control requires me to care as much about my future self as my current self.

For adults, executive control, like autobiographical memory, is closely associated with consciousness. We can act and plan and negotiate a complicated route through traffic unconsciously, mindlessly, as we say. But suppose we want to alter a plan in midstream, or to inhibit what we want to do now in favor of what we have to do in the future? That requires the conscious sense of a "me" who does the acting. Think of all those times when "you"—that is, your current self—are mindlessly but skillfully making your way back home, negotiating obstacles, turning corners, when the executive "you" suddenly springs into consciousness and realizes that today you have to go in entirely the opposite direction.

Or think of how deeply, even painfully, willpower and self-control seem to require consciousness. The executive you has to be constantly awake and alert, keeping watch over the poor, impulsive, habitual, mindless you—ready to pounce just to keep her from eating that one extra croissant or hitting the send button on that indignant e-mail.

In our everyday experience, the inner observer of consciousness, and the inner autobiographer of episodic memory, seem to be closely related to the inner executive—they seem, in fact, to be the same person: me. We feel that we have executive control because we have an überself who negotiates between our current, past, and future selves, and ultimately hands down the orders. Woody Allen vividly captures this everyday picture in *Everything You Always Wanted to Know about Sex*. Tony Randall sits in a big chair at the control center inside the hapless seducer's brain, desperately trying to coordinate the visual input on the big TV screen and the hydraulic machinery that controls his actions—"Damn, who flashed that scared expression!" As the philosopher Jerry Fodor puts it: Somebody has to be in charge so, by God, it better be me.

From a scientific point of view, of course, this can't be right. The inner executive, like the inner biographer who witnesses my memories, is what philosophers call a "homunculus"—a little man inside your head. But we can't explain what a person experiences or decides by assuming there is another littler person inside their head experiencing and deciding. Explanations like these don't explain anything—there is no überself, no inner Tony Randall in the brain, no mission control where everything gets decided.

Still, it certainly does feel that way. From a purely phenomenological point of view there does seem to be a close connection between autobiographical memory and executive control and the observing, remembering, and deciding "me"—the resident homunculus of internal consciousness. Scientific psychology tells us that we can't explain inner consciousness by saying that there really is a mysterious self that we look at with our inner eye, any more than we can explain external consciousness by saying that there really is a spotlight that sweeps over the outside world. Instead there must be a more indirect link between our capacity for autobiographical memory and executive control and the shape of our inner consciousness. Somehow, the fact that we have autobiographical memory and executive control leads us to have the experience of the inner eye and the constant self. Since autobiographical memory and executive control are so different for young children, it's likely that their internal consciousness and their sense of self are different too.

THE STREAM OF CONSCIOUSNESS

We could simply ask children what their internal consciousness is like. This is just what the Flavells did. Just as children's ideas about external awareness are very different from ours, their ideas about internal consciousness are equally peculiar. We assume that we have a stream of consciousness, that thoughts, feelings, and memories flow inexorably and constantly through our minds. But even five-year-olds don't agree. Suppose the children see Ellie, who is sitting still in a chair and staring at the wall. You ask, "Is Ellie thinking? Is anything happening in her mind right now? Is she having thoughts or feelings or ideas?" Five-year-olds deny it—if she isn't doing anything or looking at anything her mind must be a blank.

Even more surprisingly, children think the same thing about their own minds. If you ask them whether they can keep their minds totally blank for hours they confidently say yes. They continue to say this even in circumstances when it's clear to us that they must have been thinking. For example, suppose you get four-year-olds to listen to a bell ring every thirty seconds. Then the bell doesn't ring. The children are startled. But if you ask them what they were just thinking they say, "Nothing." Even more amazingly, if you explicitly ask them if they were thinking about the bell during the silence they still say "No." Older children, like adults, report that they were thinking about the bell, wondering why it hadn't rung, or waiting for it to ring again. The young children believe that you yourself think only when there is something right there to think about, just as Ellie thinks only when she is actually looking at something. One four-year-old summarized it this way: "Every time you think for a little while, something goes on and something goes off. Sometimes something goes on for a couple of minutes and then for a few minutes there is nothing going on." This is very different from the adult picture of a constant stream of consciousness.

Moreover, these young children deny experiencing visual imagery or inner speech, although they understand perfectly what a picture or a sentence is like. Suppose you say to children, "I want you to answer a question in your head, but don't say the answer out loud. Where would you find a toothbrush in your house?" Most of us do this by picturing the different rooms of the house, and then discovering the toothbrush in the bathroom. Then you ask the children if they were imagining the bathroom. Four-year-olds say no, they weren't thinking about the bathroom, although they get the answer right if you then ask them to say it out loud.

They also say you can't talk to yourself in your head. The Flavells asked them to think about how their teacher's name sounded. They denied that there was any voice in their head do-ing the naming, and if you explicitly asked them they were as likely to say that there was a picture in their head as a voice.

Preschoolers do seem to understand other aspects of thinking perfectly well. They know that if you decide something or pretend something or solve a problem you think about what you are doing. If Ellie is staring at a magic coin trick they say she is thinking about how the trick works. If you ask her whether she'd like Chi-nese or Indian food for dinner, and she says "Hmm" and sits con-templatively, they say she is thinking about where to go for dinner. They get the idea of thinking about something; they even under-stand that you can think about something without doing anything. But they don't understand that your thoughts can be internally generated. They don't understand that thoughts can simply follow the logic of your internal experience instead of being triggered from the outside.

LIVING IN THE MOMENT

What does all this tell us about what it is like to be a baby? Babies—unlike, say, H.M., the amnesic patient—can consciously remem-ber specific past events, differentiate them from current events, and retain those memories for months. They can also plan, imagining ways that the world might be and turning those possible worlds into reality.

However, babies and young children don't yet have autobiographical memory and executive control. They don't experience their lives as a single timeline stretching back into the past and forward into the future. They don't send themselves backward and forward along this timeline as adults do, recapturing for a moment that past self who was the miserable loser or the happy lover, or anticipating the despairs and joys of the future. And they don't feel immersed in a constant stream of changing thoughts and feelings.

In fact, for babies and young children there doesn't seem to be the same kind of "me" making these projections into the past and future. They don't keep track of their past mental states. While they remember that something happened, they don't seem to remember what they thought or felt about it. And although they can plan for the immediate future, they also don't seem to anticipate their future states. They don't project what they will think and feel later on.

Even very young babies have some sense of self. They can recognize themselves in a mirror and distinguish themselves from other people. The three-year-olds, after all, know that that is Johnny in the video and not some other kid. But they don't seem to have the experience of the inner observer, the autobiographer, the executive in the way that adults do.

So what is it like to be this way? I think that young children's consciousness includes all the elements of adult consciousness. There are images of past events, visions of intended goals, counterfactuals like the bizarre fantasies of pretend play, even abstract thoughts. Children can recognize the difference between these types of mental events, between present perceptions and past memories, current fantasies and future goals. But for three-year-olds these events aren't organized into a single timeline, with memories in the past and intentions in the future (and fictions and fantasies off to one side). And children may not have the experience of a single inner executive. Instead, the memories, images, and thoughts pop in and out of consciousness as they are cued by present events, or by other memories, images, and thoughts.

If for adults external consciousness is like a spotlight, internal consciousness is like a path. It is my own particular path, the track that I make as I move through the world. I can look back at it and see where I've been and look forward to peer, however dimly, toward my destination. The path pulls us forward and gives our lives their peculiar momentum. This path can, of course, easily become a rut, a narrow track that we endlessly and obsessively traverse.

Just as attention in children is more like a lantern, their inner consciousness may be more like wandering than voyaging—a journey of exploration rather than conquest. They paddle in the pond of consciousness instead of coursing down that rushing stream. Safe in the protected compass of immaturity, they can go anywhere they want. Pooing elephants over here! Weird machines that you touch with your head right this way! Now a quick detour to the rocket ship at the science center, a zigzag to touch base with Charlie Ravioli, and a beeline for the vision of the really wonderful tower I'll make with these blocks.

INTERNAL CONSCIOUSNESS, FREE ASSOCIATION, HYPNAGOGIC THOUGHT, AND INSIGHT MEDITATION

I suggested in the last chapter that we could get an empathetic glimpse of babies' external consciousness through travel or open awareness meditation. Although focused attention is the canonical example of adult external consciousness, there are many other kinds of awareness even in adults. In the same way, although the focused inner monologue of plans and memories is the canonical example of our inner experience, there are other adult experiences that may be more like the experience of young children. We may be able to get a glimpse of babies' inner consciousness through adult experiences like the "free association" of psychoanalysis, or the kind of "hypnagogic" thought we experience as we fall asleep. Before we lose consciousness altogether a stream of images, thoughts, and feelings flows through our minds. (As an incorrigible insomniac I've sometimes had the experience of briefly pulling out of the hypnagogic state and thinking, "Wait a minute, that last thought made absolutely no sense, thank God, I must be falling asleep"—the last gasp of that persistent inner observer holding on to consciousness when she really wants to release it.) Some types of "insight" meditation intentionally cultivate a similar state. Meditators try simply to observe the shifting contents of their minds without trying to control them.

In all these experiences we either deliberately or accidentally give up control of our thoughts—we intentionally turn off autobiographical memory and executive control, or we simply lose them as we doze off. But, unlike travel or open awareness meditation, in these experiences we turn inward rather than outward. In all these cases, our consciousness becomes surprisingly fragmented and labile, shifting from image to memory to thought without much apparent rhyme or reason. But it also becomes surprisingly rich; we may be startled to see how rare and strange the contents of our minds can be. The image of a convoluted purple flower morphs into a childhood memory of hiding under the table, which transforms into a sudden sensation of formless anxiety. Just as turning off the attentional spotlight can make us realize the variety and richness of our external perceptions, turning off executive control can make us realize the surprising variety of our internal experience. We can let our minds wander, as we say, and see where they go.

However valuable and interesting they may be, however, these experiences are very different from the experiences that are characteristic of everyday adult internal consciousness, and that reflect some of our most important adult abilities. In these states of consciousness the mind doesn't formulate coherent multiparagraph logical arguments or make step-by-step plans for all the contingencies of the child-care building project, or lovingly replay last weekend moment by moment from Friday to Sunday. You can't or at least don't do any of these things when you are engaged in free association or hypnagogic thought or insight meditation. Children don't seem to do this sort of focused long-range planning or systematic recollection either.

Moreover, the sense of a single conscious "I" seems to become at least attenuated in these childlike states. The inner observer fades away. Indeed, one of the insights of the insight-meditation tradition is supposed to be precisely that there is no "I." Whether or not this is true for adults, it does seem plausible that it is true for babies and very young children.

WHY DOES CONSCIOUSNESS CHANGE?

By the time they are six or so children seem to have developed the basics of autobiographical memory, executive control, and the inner observer. They have a roughly adult understanding of consciousness, too. What causes these changes in inner consciousness?

The development of language almost certainly plays a role. Autobiographical memory and executive control are developing in tandem with the ability to use language, which provides us with a medium for telling ourselves, as well as others, what happened and what to do. Recall the children who went to the zoo and remembered only what their mothers had told them about the animals and their adventures. It is also striking that for adults this inner linguistic monologue—the constant babble of inner speech—is one of the most important and characteristic features of internal consciousness. But Flavell's findings suggest that for children inner speech is much less prominent.

Language certainly plays a role in our adult consciousness. That inner voice nags and urges and instructs and persuades us. There is another possibly apocryphal story about the philosopher Jerry Fodor (he's the Yogi Berra of philosophy). Someone asked what his stream of consciousness was like as he wrote philosophy. His reply was that it mostly said, "Come on, Jerry, you can do it, Jerry, keep going, Jerry." We all seem to have those inner voices. But for children that voice at least seems less hectoring. After all, they have the real voice of their parents to direct them and restrict them and generally keep them on target and out of trouble.

These differences in the internal consciousness of adults and children, like the differences in their external consciousness, reflect the general division of labor between children and grown-ups. Children's characteristic consciousness is shaped by their characteristic agenda—learn as much about the world as you can as quickly as you can. Take source amnesia, suggestibility, and the purging of past false beliefs. Suppose you just want to update your beliefs as quickly and efficiently as possible. It makes sense to simply discard your past false beliefs, and not to retain information about where those beliefs came from.

This is especially true if, like babies, you are constantly updating and changing many of your beliefs at once. Babies and young children learn so much so quickly that their entire stock of knowledge turns over every few months—they go through whole paradigm shifts between their third and fourth birthday. We saw in chapter 3 that children are constantly learning and creating brand-new causal maps of the world. In developmental psychology we talk breezily about the big differences between nine-month-olds' and twelve-month-olds' conceptions of objects, or three-year-olds' and four-year-olds' understanding of minds. But what this means is that in just a few months, these children have completely changed their minds about what the world is like. Imagine that your worldview in September was totally different from what it was in June, and then completely changed again by Christmas. Or imagine that your most basic beliefs would be entirely transformed between 2009 and 2010, and then again by 2012. Really flexible and innovative adults might change their minds this way two or three times in a lifetime.

As we grow older our beliefs will become more and more well confirmed—we'll have gathered more and more evidence supporting them. So, quite properly, we'll be more reluctant to change them. If your agenda is not to change your beliefs, but to hold on to as many of them as possible, only changing a few of them very deliberately when you are sure you need to, you might act quite differently. Then it makes more sense to keep track of the history and sources of your beliefs. You want to change your beliefs only when you are sure the new information is robust and reliable— and more robust and reliable than the existing beliefs.

Other aspects of baby consciousness may also reflect these differences. Anecdotally, at least, there is a relation between adult states such as free association and hypnagogic consciousness, and innovation and creativity. Patients feel that they have made breakthroughs in self-understanding as they lie on the couch, and scientists report that they get great ideas in the middle of the night. And, of course, insight meditation is precisely supposed to provide insights. Even for adults, uncritical "brainstorming," a process that feels much like free association or hypnagogic thought, is a good way to encourage new ideas. Babies are all about innovation and creativity. These experiences may be the phenomenological markers of an underlying thought process that puts together ideas and information in new ways, just as vivid attention seems to be a phenomenological marker of learning and plasticity.

On the other hand, autobiographical memory and executive control both reflect our characteristically adult ability to conceive and execute long-term plans. By seeing my experience as a single coherent whole, connected in the past, present, and future, I can do things like put up with a graduate-student salary in the hope of a professorship later on, or struggle through the first pages of a book that will only be published five years later. In our evolutionary past, these abilities let us plant seeds now to establish a future harvest, or invest now in making a tool that we will only use later.

The executive-control one-cookie/two-cookie experiments were first done back in the sixties. Years later they turned out to be a remarkably good predictor of teenage success at school. Children who were more able to defer gratification when they were five years old became teenagers who were more likely to be rated as competent and mature, and their SAT scores were consistently higher than those of children who couldn't tolerate the delay.

Some psychologists have even suggested that teenagers who literally don't feel that they have a future are most likely to behave self-destructively. Michael Chandler looked at teenagers in aboriginal communities in Canada. These teenagers are notoriously at risk for suicide, as well as less drastically self-destructive actions.

Chandler found that adolescents at risk for suicide had a less coherent sense of themselves. They were less likely to connect their
current, past, and especially future selves than children who were
less at risk.

A MAP OF MYSELF: CONSTRUCTING CONSCIOUSNESS

So far I've argued that developmental cognitive science can tell us
something about what it is like to be a baby or a young child. It's
quite different from what it is like to be an adult. But can these
differences tell us something more about consciousness itself?

Thinking about children illuminates a central debate in philosophy. Is our conscious experience irrefutable, the bedrock of our
knowledge and our lives? Or is consciousness itself a construc-
tion, even a kind of illusion?

Until about a hundred years ago philosophers thought our
conscious experiences caused us to act in the way we do. If we
examined our own minds, we would see the ideas, emotions, and
decisions that made us act. That was Descartes's method, and he
argued that conscious experience was the one thing we knew
for certain. It was also the method of the earliest scientific psychologists, like Wilhelm Wundt and William James. And this kind
of introspective meditation is crucial to Asian philosophy and
psychology.

But introspection leads to troubling contradictions. When we
look at our own minds are we also changing how our minds work?
For example, do we actually experience the inner self, that extended observer, biographer, and executive, or not? David Hume
famously argued that we do not: the self is an illusion, it disappears whenever we try to look for it. The Buddhist tradition makes

a similar claim. Is this because there is no fundamentally experienced self or because the experienced self disappears when you try to look at it? Does introspection reveal your true experience, or does it change that experience into something else?

As psychological science has developed we have found more and more cases where introspection is misleading. In fact, sometimes our conscious experience is directly contradicted by our actions or other psychological evidence. In inattentional blindness, for example, we feel sure that we are consciously seeing the entire scene, and yet it turns out that we are missing the gorilla. In blindsight, patients feel that they can't see something that they can accurately reach for. In autobiographical memory, we feel sure we remember events that we never actually experienced, ranging from the details of our initial reaction to 9/11 to alien abductions. In experiences of executive control, we often feel sure we are making a rational choice when, in fact, we are in the grip of some irrational unconscious bias. And in all of these cases we experience a homunculus, the inner observer, biographer, and decider that we know just can't exist.

These contradictions have led some philosophers, notably Daniel Dennett, to argue that consciousness doesn't really exist at all. That's a pretty extreme view. But Dennett holds down one end of a continuum. This continuum runs from "anticonsciousness" philosophers such as Dennett or Paul and Patricia Churchland to "proconsciousness" philosophers such as John Searle and David Chalmers. The first camp emphasizes the changeable and contradictory nature of conscious experience. The second camp emphasizes the special first-person certainty of consciousness. For philosophers like Chalmers the gap between consciousness and the brain suggests that consciousness is immaterial, not that it is illusory. Chalmers thinks that the conscious mind and the brain are fundamentally different kinds of things, though he wouldn't identify the mind with a mystical soul.

Looking at children doesn't explain away consciousness but it does weigh in on Dennett's side of the argument. Thinking about children makes consciousness seem even more confusing and contradictory. Are children accurately reporting conscious experiences that are different from ours? Or have they just got mistaken ideas about what their consciousness is like? Do children really not remember that they thought there were candies in the box? Or are they just mistaken about their past experience? Can we be conscious at all if we don't have an inner self? What does it mean to have a conscious experience without knowing that it is *my* conscious experience? And if children can be mistaken about their own conscious experience, surely we adults can also be mistaken?

Many aspects of consciousness that we take for granted, like the idea that we know what we thought a few seconds ago, or that our consciousness is a single unbroken stream, or that we have a unified self, fall apart when we look at children. Looking at children tells us that consciousness is not a single unitary phenomenon with special features. Our vivid awareness of the external world may be different from our sense of an executive "I," which may be different from the capacity to fantasize or to recapture past events. Children are conscious but their consciousness seems very different from ours.

Looking at children also makes us appreciate the gap between conscious experience and psychological explanation. We saw in earlier chapters that children are unconsciously the most rational beings on earth, brilliantly drawing accurate conclusions from data, performing complex statistical analyses, and doing clever experiments. But these brilliantly rational learning abilities are accompanied by a kind of consciousness that looks and feels irrational.

Piaget and Freud also speculated, as I have, that children's consciousness might be like free association or hypnagogic thought. Talk a while with a three-year-old and it's hard to avoid that conclusion. But they took the further step of concluding that this was what children's actual thinking was like—irrational, incoherent, and solipsistic. And that clearly isn't true. That may be what a three-year-old mind feels like but it isn't what a three-year-old mind really is like. The gap between the way the mind functions and the shape of conscious experience is even greater for children than for adults.

Looking at how consciousness changes also emphasizes the complex and indirect interactions among what we think, what we know, and what we experience. Children's consciousness changes because they learn more about the world and about how their own minds work. When they begin to understand that other people's desires or beliefs may change, for example, they start to experience those changes themselves. Looking at children suggests that there is a constant interweaving between largely unconscious processes of learning and the detailed texture of our conscious experience. When we change the way we think, we also change the way thinking feels to us. When what we know changes, our experience changes too. Consciousness isn't a transparent and lucid Cartesian stream. Instead it's a turbulent, muddy mess. Philosophers may have to resign themselves to just playing in the mud for a while yet. At least children can tell us it might be fun.

6.

Heraclitus' River and the Romanian Orphans

HOW DOES OUR EARLY LIFE SHAPE OUR LATER LIFE?

*

Heraclitus, one of the very first recorded philosophers, questioned whether we stay the same throughout life. Recall his famous aphorism that a man never steps in the same river twice because neither the river nor the man are the same. The nature of our personal identity, whether and how we remain the same person over time, is a classic philosophical question. Philosophy is often as much about stories as arguments, and the problem of identity has led to some wonderful stories.

One story is the tale of Ulysses and the sirens. Ulysses knows that the siren song will lure him to his death but, consumed by his characteristic curiosity, he wants to hear it anyway. So he has his sailors tie him to the mast of his ship, and gets them to fill their ears with wax so that they won't be influenced by the sirens themselves and won't hear anything he says. He commands them to keep sailing forward. Sure enough, as soon as he hears the song, he curses his earlier precautions and commands his men to untie him; but the men, deaf to his commands, obliviously sail on. The question is, what does Ulysses want? Does he want to be untied or not? It seems almost as if the earlier Ulysses and the Ulysses who hears the sirens are two different people.

The philosopher Derek Parfit tells an even more troubling version of this story. "In several years, a young Russian will inherit vast estates. Because he has socialist ideals he intends, now, to give the land to the peasants. But he knows that in time his ideals may fade. To guard against this possibility, he first signs a legal document, which will automatically give away the land, and which can be revoked only with his wife's consent. He then says to his wife, 'Promise me that if I ever change my mind, and ask you to revoke this document, you will not consent.' He adds, 'I regard my ideals as essential to me. If I lose those ideals I want you to think that I cease to exist. I want you to regard your husband then, not as me, the man who asks you for this promise, but only as his corrupted later self. Promise me that you would not do what he asks.'" Sure enough, later, when he inherits the land he insists that his wife revoke the document as a relic of his youthful folly. What should she do?

And here is another even more disturbing tale from Parfit. Scientists have finally discovered a way to offer you immortality. They raise a set of clones, perfect young physical bodies. When you get old, they duplicate all of your neural circuitry in the brain of one of those clones, they make the brain identical to yours in every respect, matching all your memories and thoughts and feelings. Then they kill you. Would you accept this offer?

These philosophical stories all vividly raise the question of what makes me *me*. In what sense do I remain the same throughout my life? What are the relationships among all the phases of my existence, the young rebel, the old conservative, Ulysses before and after the temptation of the sirens?

In the last chapter, we saw that even very young children, four or five years old, already have a single autobiographical story that links their past and their future. They know that the "I" who wore the sticker in the past is the same as the "I" watching the video now, and the "I" who might need sunglasses in the desert in the future. This identity doesn't just emerge automatically, though. Instead, children actively create that "I"—that sense that they are the unique protagonist of their own autobiography. In fact, in the deferred-gratification experiments children are starting to be able to act like Ulysses, with cookies as the sirens. They can frustrate their current selves in the interest of their future selves.

These cases involve short time spans—putting together the "I" right now with the "I" of a few minutes ago or a few minutes to come. When we look at the long scale of an entire life, the questions become even more acute. It's hard enough for children to work out the relationship between the present self and the self of a few minutes ago. It's even harder to unify my present self and the self of forty years ago. And yet we live our lives as if there is a single story that makes the child father to the man—that unites childhood and adulthood. In fact, that story feels like an essential part of our personal identity. Knowing how we were will tell us how we are now.

How do our early childhood experiences influence our lives later on? These questions, more than any others, dominate public and private discussions of childhood. What did my parents do right (or more often wrong) to make me the person I am today? What can I do to ensure that my child turns out well?

Our everyday intuitions about these questions veer wildly. We all feel that what happened to us when we were children shapes who we are now. This is one reason that Freudian ideas continue to be so popular, in spite of the fact that many of them have been discredited scientifically. This intuition may also be responsible for the popularity of self-help and parenting books, and it even underlies the enthusiasm for grim and depressing childhood memoirs.

On the other hand, we also feel that later events can override the influence of childhood. A happy marriage or a fortunate vocation or even a good friend can rescue us from early misery. More powerfully, we believe that we can actively shape our lives in a way that allows us to escape from childhood determinism. The memoirs of childhood unhappiness are more likely to have an uplifting ending, a celebration of the possibility of "recovery," than they are to have an equally unhappy conclusion. (There is, of course, a striking dearth of memoirs that describe how, in spite of a wonderful childhood and warm and loving parents, the author of his own free will made himself into a rotten grown-up.)

Philosophers, preoccupied with the troubles of Ulysses and the Russian nobleman, haven't paid as much attention to these questions about childhood. This is too bad because a little philosophical clarity would be helpful. There are a number of ways to think about early childhood and its impact on later life and they often get confused. We might think that certain childhood events simply cause us to have certain adult characteristics. Alternatively, we might think that our experiences as children cause us to have certain kinds of beliefs about the world and other people, and those beliefs shape our adult thought and action.

As we'll see, there is some evidence for both these views but the scientific picture is complicated. The complications emerge precisely because of our human capacities for change. Our ability to change our environment makes the relation between childhood and adulthood especially intricate and complex.

There is also a more subtle but important way that early childhood influences our adult lives. Because of autobiographical memory and our sense of self, my childhood simply is, for good or ill, part of what I am as an adult. It isn't that my childhood causes me to be an adult of a particular kind—it's that what I am as an adult includes my childhood.

LIFE CYCLES

Are there particular childhood events—especially things that parents do or don't do—that directly influence our later lives? When I give talks to parents, at least three-quarters of the questions I get are along these lines: If I let my child watch TV will she have attention problems? If I read to her in the womb will she be smarter? If I play Mozart will he do better in math class? Or (more generally) if I do x (work/don't work, let him sleep in my bed/don't let him sleep in my bed, let him cry/don't let him cry) will he end up as a hopeless neurotic? This is often half, but only half, ironically phrased as "What will he tell his shrink about me?"

These questions are irresistible—I've been asking myself the same questions about my children for thirty years. But there is surprisingly little scientific evidence for this simple view of the effects of early experience on later life. Take a particularly striking and sad example: the children who were abandoned in Romanian orphanages during the tyrannical regime of Nicolae Ceauşescu. Although these children weren't physically abused, they suffered terrible social and emotional deprivation. No one played with them or held them or talked to them or loved them. Babies lay alone in their cribs for hours, indeed days and weeks, at a time.

After the regime fell and the horror of the orphanages was discovered, many of these children, by then three or four years old, were adopted and taken into British middle-class homes. They looked completely different from other children. They were physically much smaller, they appeared to be severely retarded, they barely talked, and their social behavior was bizarre.

And yet by the time the children were six they had largely caught up. Their average IQ was only a little lower than a similar group of more fortunate children. They loved their adoptive parents in the same way that other children love their parents. In fact, most of the Romanian orphans were completely indistinguishable from other children.

Some of the children, though, continued to suffer. Although these children had recovered compared with their pitiful beginnings, they still seemed to lag behind other children both cognitively and socially. The longer the children had been in the orphanages, the more likely they were to have problems later, and the more severe the problems were likely to be. This suggests that the early experiences really were responsible for the later problems. So the story of the Romanian orphans is a story both of resilience, for all those children who recovered completely, and of risk, for those children who didn't.

The Romanian orphans are a dramatic case in two ways: they were dramatically deprived as babies, and their circumstances changed equally dramatically when they were adopted. But this combination of risk and resilience is the moral of studies of more typical development as well. Being abused as a child makes you more likely to abuse your own children, but the overwhelming majority of abused children don't become abusive parents. Somehow they escape from the circumstances of their early lives.

THE PARADOX OF INHERITANCE

You might think this means that, in fact, childhood experience has no influence at all on later life, and that most of what we are is shaped by our genes. But this doesn't seem to be true either. Instead, we see so much variation in development because our genetic inheritance and our experience interact. By itself, this is a banal observation. It's more interesting to see how complex and multifaceted those interactions can be.

Psychologists often talk about "heritability." People growing up in the same environment can vary in how smart or how sane or how miserable they are—in what psychologists call their "traits." Then you can ask if there is a mathematical relationship between these similarities and differences in traits and genetic similarities and differences. If you're smarter, or crazier, or sadder than other kids, were your parents likely to be smarter or crazier or sadder than other parents? How much of the difference between people on some individual trait is predictable from the differences in their genes?

Twin studies are a particularly good way to do this. We know that identical twins share all the same genes while fraternal twins don't, but both fraternal and identical twins share the same environment. If identical twins are more similar on some trait than fraternal twins, that indicates that the trait is "heritable." For example, if one identical twin is alcoholic, there's a good chance that the other twin will also suffer from alcoholism. If the twin is fraternal, there is less of a chance, though the fraternal twin is still more likely to be alcoholic than a random unrelated person.

Another technique is to look at adopted children. Are adopted children more similar on some trait to their birth parents, who share the same genes, or to their adoptive parents, who share the same environment? Again, children with alcoholic birth parents, who are adopted by people who aren't alcoholics, are more likely to suffer from alcoholism themselves than other similar people without that genetic background. You can also just measure these traits in a group of parents and then in their children. People with alcoholism are more likely to have alcoholic parents than people with other kinds of problems. So alcoholism is heritable.

Using these techniques, some psychologists propose a precise number that indicates the heritability of some trait. Based on the kinds of studies I just described, psychologists may say that in a standard white, middle-class group of people, the sort of people included in these studies, alcoholism has a heritability of .40. Similarly, you can measure the heritability of IQ in a standard white, middle-class group of people. The correlation between variation in IQ scores and variation in genes in that sort of group is estimated to be between .40 and .70. Even a heritability of .40 is pretty substantial.

People often assume that very heritable traits must be due to genes while less heritable traits are due to environment. These kinds of studies underlie the headlines about "genes for" everything from criminality to creativity. But heritability measures variation within a certain environment, and human beings create their own environments, particularly their own social environments— many of the environments they create are unlike any that have gone before. We've seen that our (genetically determined) capacities for counterfactual thought and causal intervention mean that we can act on our environment to make it a different environment. This is the rule rather than the exception in human life. The trouble is that the very same genes may have very different effects in that new environment than they did in the old one. This makes it conceptually difficult to sort out the effects of genes and the effects of the environment.

Take a very simple and striking case. When babies are born in hospitals they're immediately tested for a rare genetic disorder called phenylketonuria, or PKU. Children with PKU are unable to metabolize certain chemicals in food. If they have a normal diet they become severely retarded, but if they get a special diet that avoids these chemicals they are fine. So the mental retardation of PKU is absolutely 100 percent due to genes and it is also absolutely 100 percent due to environment. It was completely heritable when the chemicals were always present and it is not heritable at all now that they can be removed.

Human beings have used their innate cognitive abilities to discover the causal link between PKU and retardation and have intervened to change the environment of children with the defective genes. For other animals, without these abilities, the effects of PKU would indeed be entirely due to genetics. But for us they are not.

You can also see these paradoxes of heritability in more ordinary cases. For example, Eric Turkheimer at the University of Virginia discovered a database of very poor twins. All the earlier twin studies involved middle-class children. It turns out that IQ is far more heritable for rich children than for poor children. In fact, for poor children the effect of genes on IQ almost disappears—there is little correlation between how smart parents are and how smart their children are, and identical twins' IQ is no more similar than that of fraternal twins. So it seems that poor children's IQ is less affected by their genes than rich children's IQ. But how can that be? Surely poverty can't change your DNA?

The answer is that small variations in a poor child's environment—going to a better or worse school, for example—make a big difference to their IQ. Those differences swamp any genetic differences. Rich children are generally already going to good schools, so the differences between them are more likely to reflect genetic variation. Notoriously, Charles Murray and Richard Herrnstein in their book *The Bell Curve* suggested that the heritability of IQ of for me, and how good he always was; and at last I struck the time I saved him by telling the men we had small-pox aboard, and he was so grateful, and said I was the best friend old Jim ever had in the world, and the ONLY one he's got now; and then I happened to look around and see that paper.

It was a close place. I took it up, and held it in my hand. I was a-trembling, because I'd got to decide, forever, betwixt two things, and I knowed it. I studied a minute, sort of holding my breath, and then says to myself:

"All right, then, I'll GO to hell"—and tore it up.

9.
Babies and the Meaning of Life

*

I love Christmas and have always celebrated it with particular fervor and intensity. Every year, neglecting final exams, faculty meetings, and grant submission deadlines, I decorate a big tree, put swags on the mantelpieces, bake gingerbread houses, roast geese, sing carols, and spend far too much on stocking stuffers—the works. For almost all my life I've had children at home and that has made Christmas especially rich, even if it came with the ambivalence of so much parenting. There was great egocentric pleasure in the doing itself, even more pleasure in thinking how much the children liked it, just a little edge of exhaustion at the effort and just a smidgen of doubt about whether the children really appreciated it enough.

I love Christmas so much in spite of the fact that my great-grandfather was a devout and distinguished rabbi, and I was raised as an equally devout atheist. I resolve the apparent contradiction by telling people that I love Christmas because, above all, it's a holiday that celebrates birth and children—the most moving

Christmas carols are both hymns and lullabies. I can't think of anything more worthy of celebration.

In this book, I've argued that thinking about children can help solve some deep and ancient philosophical questions—questions about imagination, truth, and consciousness, and also identity, love, and morality. But beyond even these questions are what we might call the meaning-of-life questions—more broadly philosophical or even spiritual and religious questions that academic philosophers like me rarely tackle. What makes life meaningful, beautiful, and morally significant? Is there something that we care about more than we care about ourselves? What endures beyond death?

For most parents, in day-to-day, simple, ordinary life, there is an obvious answer to these questions—even if it isn't the only answer. Our children give point and purpose to our lives. They are beautiful (with a small dispensation for chicken pox, scraped knees, and runny noses), and the words and images they create are beautiful too. They are at the root of our deepest moral dilemmas and greatest moral triumphs. We care more about our children than we do about ourselves. Our children live on after we are gone, and this gives us a kind of immortality.

Curiously, though these feelings are so pervasive, they're rarely even considered in philosophy and theology. In fact, it was thinking about immortality that first made me notice the missing children in philosophy. When I was ten, I read Plato for the first time and it changed my life. I still vividly remember the battered Penguin paperback that made me want to become a philosopher. But even in that very first encounter with philosophy there was a catch. The argument in the Penguin Plato that impressed me the most was Socrates' case for immortality in the *Phaedo*. Like many ten-year-olds—or fifty-year-olds, for that matter—I was existentially terrified by death and was certainly in the market for a good argument for immortality. Socrates argues that something as complex as the soul can't appear and vanish out of nowhere, and therefore it must exist, before and after our individual lives, in an abstract Platonic heaven.

What struck me about the argument was that there was no mention anywhere of children. It seemed obvious to me that your soul was created, at least in part, by the genes you inherited and the ideas you acquired from your parents, and that it continued after death in the genes and ideas you passed on to your children. Of course, this idea depended on scientific concepts that weren't available to Socrates. But even if Socrates didn't know about genes, he definitely knew about children. I'll admit that attaining immortality through your children isn't necessarily the answer to Socrates' question. But he could have at least mentioned it as a possibility.

Nor did children appear in the 2,500 years of philosophy to come. Many profound questions about human nature can be answered by thinking about children. And thinking about children raises new and profound questions itself. Most parents, and even alloparents, feel that children help give their lives meaning. Yet children have been almost invisible to the deepest thinkers in human history.

There is an obvious historical explanation for this—Socrates was a man, like nearly all the philosophers and theologians who followed him. Children have always been part of women's realm. Like most other aspects of life that are associated with women, they were not the sort of thing philosophers talked about.

But the problem may run deeper. Perhaps our intuitions about children really are too parochial and personal to be genuinely profound. My children are *mine*, after all. My feeling for them doesn't have the universal character that we expect from spiritual intuitions. They seem beautiful to me, but then mothers love even a face that only a mother could love. From an evolutionary point of view, too, those intuitions might just be an illusion. Of course, you feel that your own children are important—it's just another evolutionary trick that genes use to reproduce themselves. Your genes might make you really want to take care of the children who share those genes. But this doesn't have anything to do with the meaning of life.

This is part of the deeper question that haunts all scientists who think about spirituality. Human beings have characteristic emotions of awe and wonder, moral worth and aesthetic profundity. They have a sense of meaning and purpose, and an intuition that there is something larger than themselves. But do these emotions and intuitions capture something real about the world? From a scientific perspective, these emotions and beliefs, like all emotions and beliefs, are the result of activity in our brains and have an evolutionary history. Often this is taken to mean that they are illusory—or at least that they don't have the significance they appear to have.

In fact, my brain is designed to tell me the truth, at least most of the time. When I look at the desk in front of me, my belief that the desk is there is entirely due to activity in my brain—activity that has a long evolutionary history. But there really *is* a desk there and my brain activity accurately tells me about it. I can use that information as a guide to real actions in the real world—I can put my teacup down there without spilling it. When I look down from the edge of a cliff, I feel fear. I can tell you how my evolutionary history and the activity in my brain generate that feeling, but that doesn't mean the feeling is just an illusion. On the contrary, I *should* feel fear—my brain is telling me something terribly important about the world and my relation to it. The fact that a belief is the result of evolutionary processes that shaped my brain makes it more likely to be true, not less so. Evolution tracks the real world.

On the other hand, there are perceptions, emotions, and beliefs that really are just bits of faulty wiring, mind bugs. When the moon looks larger at the horizon than at the apex of the sky, or seems to be following my car, or appears to have a face, those really are illusions. We know something about how the brain creates those illusions. When I see a harmless garter snake and recoil in horror, that really is a mistake left over from my evolutionary past. So the great question isn't whether spiritual intuitions are in our brains—of course they are. The question is whether they're simply a bit of deceptive brain wiring or whether they tell us something important, valuable, and true about the world and ourselves. Are they like seeing the man in the moon or seeing the teacup on the desk?

I don't know about the spiritual intuitions that accompany mystical experiences or religious ceremonies. But I do think that the sense of significance that accompanies the experience of raising children isn't just an evolutionarily determined illusion, like the man in the moon or the terrifying garter snake. Children really do put us in touch with important, real, and universal aspects of the human condition.

AWE

Like most scientists, I doubt that there is some ultimate, transcendent, foundational purpose to our lives, or to the universe, whether we interpret this in terms of a personal God or a mystical metaphysics. But certainly we can point to sources of real meaning in our actual human lives as we live them.

One classic kind of spiritual intuition is awe: our sense of the richness and complexity of the universe outside our own immediate concerns. It's the experience of standing outside on a dark night and gazing up at the infinite multitude of stars. This kind of awe is the scientific emotion par excellence. Many scientists who are otherwise atheists point to it as a profound, deep, and significant reward of their work. Scientists are certainly subject to ambition, the lust for fame, the desire for power, and other dubious motivations. Still, I think all scientists, even the most domineering Harvard silverbacks, are also moved by this kind of pure amazement at how much there is to learn about the world.

I've argued that babies and young children experience this kind of feeling, this lantern consciousness, all the time. They may feel this way gazing up at a Mickey Mouse mobile instead of at the Milky Way, but the experience is very much the same. And it's more than just a feeling for both the scientists and the children. The universe at every level, from Mickey Mouse to the Milky Way and beyond, is indeed wonderfully rich and complex and, well, just awesome. And our capacity to appreciate this richness is entirely genuine. Not everybody engages in science or even cares about it—but almost everybody shares in the learning of young children.

MAGIC

A second and rather different kind of spiritual intuition, what we might call our sense of magic, is our feeling that there are also possible worlds beyond the world we know. There are worlds of the imagination, worlds that are quite different from ours, magic, unreal worlds. The earliest recorded human stories are myths and legends, wild tales of faraway counterfactuals. Grey-eyed Athena, Pele the volcano goddess, and Thor the thunder hurler are as unlikely as Dunzer or Charlie Ravioli or Gawkin the Dinosaur. The restrained and realistic imaginary creatures of novels are relatively modern creations.

These stories—expressions of magic, myth, and metaphor—have always been closely connected to a different kind of spiritual sense, a different intuition that the world is wider than we are. Explicitly religious writers such as C. S. Lewis and J. R. R. Tolkien link religion and magic. They point to the wonder and richness of the fairy tales we tell children, and children tell us. And, of course, both Lewis and Tolkien wrote stories that captured that sense of possibility, that sense that an alternate universe might lurk in every wardrobe. Those stories were aimed at children, but they speak equally to adults. In their pretend play, young children explore the magic of human possibility in a particularly wide-ranging and creative way. Their liberation from mundane cares lets them move into the world of the possible with particular ease.

This sense of possibility isn't an illusion. The human world really is rich with magical potential in a very concrete and realistic way. I can watch *Beauty and the Beast*, the quintessentially magical Jean Cocteau fairy tale, on my computer, Skyping with my distant son at the same time. As Beauty looks into the magic mirror that sends her visions of her loved ones, I can stare into the real images in the real magic mirror of my laptop, images that once existed only in the minds of imaginative geeks.

Stories can also create new ways for human beings to live, as well as new worlds for them to live in. Religious stories do this, in particular, whether they are parables or koans, tales of Valhalla or Chelm. By imagining alternative minds, alternative ways that people might think and act, human beings can transform themselves and their communities. The sense of magical possibility that is so vivid in children is also at the root of much that is real and important about our lives. And the space of human imaginative possibilities really is much wider than any individual mind can capture.

LOVE

Children can also tell us, more than anything else, about the spiritual intuitions that we might call love. Our love for our children, and our children's love for us, has a special quality. I said before that the particularity of our feelings about children might make them seem spiritually dubious. But the love we feel for children, not just mother love but the father love of social monogamy and the babysitter/sibling/grandmother/next-door-neighbor love of the alloparent, has a special quality of both particularity and universality. It is a powerful model for the love that underpins religious and moral intuitions.

One of the everyday but astonishing facts of life is that while we choose our friends and our mates, we don't choose our children. When we give birth to a baby, and even when, as an alloparent, we take on the care of a baby we haven't borne, we have no idea what that baby will be like. I may hope that my baby combines the best features of myself and my mate, while I fear that he actually combines the worst ones. Still, given the genetic lottery of human mating, and the contingencies of human nurturing, the most likely outcome is that the jumbled-up genes of each individual will come out looking like nothing else on earth. Even the most basic features of what a baby is like are beyond our control, a situation that becomes vivid for the parents of children with disabilities.

And yet, with some tragic exceptions, caregivers love the babies they care for. Sometimes they love the neediest babies, the babies with Down syndrome and cerebral palsy and cystic fibrosis, most of all. And even more oddly, when we care for a child we love *that* child, not some arbitrary notion of children in general. We love our children just for the particular characteristics that we couldn't possibly have anticipated—my oldest son's intensity, talent, and straight-backed confidence; my middle son's brown curls, wit, and intelligence; my youngest's luminous smile, warm blue eyes, and sensitivity. In fact, these lists don't capture it either— I just love *them*, not even because they are my children, but just because they are Alexei, Nicholas, and Andres.

Even more paradoxically, yet even more profoundly, our love for our children is inversely related to the benefits they provide us. Even with mates, and certainly with friends, we expect a certain reciprocity—I'll take care of your neuroses if you'll tolerate mine. The neediest of our intimates gives us something in return. But *every* child is needier than the most intolerably demanding friend or lover.

Imagine a novel in which a woman took in a stranger who was unable to walk or talk or even eat by himself. She fell completely in love with him at first sight, fed and clothed and washed him, gradually helped him to become competent and independent, spent more than half her income on him, nursed him through sickness, and thought about him more than about anything else. And after twenty years of this she helped him find a young wife and move far away. You couldn't bear the sappiness of it. But that, quite simply, is just about every mother's story. And it's also the story of every human community—every constellation of mothers and fathers and socially monagomous mates, every group of siblings and babysitters and alloparents. It's not so much that we care for children because we love them as that we love them because we care for them.

These moral intuitions about childrearing aren't captured in most philosophical traditions. The classic philosophical moral views—utilitarian or Kantian, libertarian or socialist—are rooted in intuitions about good and harm, autonomy and reciprocity, individuality and universality. Each individual person deserves to pursue happiness and avert harm, and by cooperating reciprocally we can maximize the good of everyone—the basic idea of the social contract. But individualist, universalist, and contractual moral systems just don't seem to capture our intuitions about raising kids.

On the other hand, this combination of particularity and selflessness is much like the love and concern that are part of our spiritual intuitions. We capture it in stories of saints and bodhisattvas and tzaddikim. They are supposed to feel that combination of singular, transparent, particular affection and selfless concern for *everybody*. No real human can do that. And, of course, there are many ways to approach that ideal and to care for others— ways that don't involve children. Still, caring for children is an awfully fast and efficient way to experience at least a little saintliness.

CONCLUSION

We can return to the questions we started at the beginning of this book. How is it possible for human beings to change? What does this tell us about children and childhood, especially very young children and very early childhood? There are three intertwined strands in the answer—learning, counterfactuals, and caregiving, or more poetically, truth, imagination, and love. In science and philosophy these three aspects of human experience are often treated as if they were quite separate from one another—epistemology, aesthetics, and ethics all have very different traditions. But for young children truth, imagination, and love are inextricably intertwined.

Truth, first. We change what we do as we learn more about what the world is like. Human beings can learn more than any other animal and that's one reason they can change more than any other animal. Children are born knowing a lot about the world and other people. That knowledge gives them a head start in learning new things about the particular world they live in and the particular set of people they share it with. But, at the end of the day, they may even learn to overthrow the assumptions they started with.

Babies love to learn. They learn by simply observing the unfolding statistics of the events around them. They are open to all the richness of the wide world. They pay attention to anything new and unexpected—anything they might learn from—but they also actively do things to learn. When they play, children actively experiment on the world and they use the results of those experiments to change what they think. The statistics they observe and the experiments they perform help them to make new causal maps of the world around them.

Children don't just learn about the physical world. They also learn about the psychological world. They learn what the people around them are like. Since human cultures can change, this means that what children learn about people can also change. Children learn the psychology of those around them—their particular combination of beliefs, desires, and feelings, personality traits, motivations, and interests. But they also learn the normative aspects of human psychology. They rapidly learn the rules that those around them follow, both the arbitrary conventions and the moral principles.

And children don't just learn about other people—they learn about themselves. Literally, from the time they are born they link their own feelings to those of others. They use what they learn about other people to learn about themselves and vice versa. Children begin to see how understanding your own mind can help you to change what you do—how, for example, closing your eyes can help you resist that cookie. They also start to use their psychological understanding to make a unified and coherent story of their own experiences, a story that continues through all the twists and turns of human life.

This remarkable ability to find the truth, in turn, depends on the capacity to imagine and to love. The Bayesian theory of learning depends on the idea that children can imagine alternatives to their current picture of the world. Children construct alternative hypotheses about what the world is like, they compare and contrast different possible causal maps of the world. And a fundamental principle of this kind of learning is that even the most unlikely possibilities may eventually turn out to be true.

And babies can devote their attention and action to learning because they depend on the care of the people around them. Because we love babies, they can learn. Even more significantly, one of the central ways that babies and children learn is by watching what the people they love do and listening to what they say. This kind of learning allows children to take advantage of the discoveries of the previous generations. Caregivers implicitly and unconsciously teach babies at the same time that they care for them.

If imagination helps children to find the truth, finding the truth also increases the power of the imagination. Very young children can use their causal maps of the world—their theories—to imagine different ways that the world might be. They can think about counterfactual possibilities. As those theories change, as children learn and their ideas about the world become more and more accurate, the counterfactuals they can produce and the possibilities they can envision become richer and richer. These counterfactuals let children create different worlds and they underpin the great flowering of pretend play in early childhood. Eventually, they enable even adults to imagine alternative ways the world could be and make those alternatives real.

Causal maps also apply to minds as well as things. And that means that children can imagine counterfactual people, like imaginary companions, as well as counterfactual worlds. This lets children interact with people in new and more complex ways. And it lets them, and us, create new social conventions and moral rules that will bring about better outcomes.

So imagination depends on knowledge, but it also depends on love and care. Just as children can learn so freely because they are protected by adults, they can imagine so freely because they are loved. More, counterfactual thinking necessarily has a normative element—imagining the future also means evaluating which futures you should bring about. From the time they are very young children root these decisions in moral responses. They try to do good and avoid harm. And those responses are themselves rooted in the deeply empathic, intimate, and literally selfless interactions between babies and caregivers.

Finally, love itself depends on knowledge and imagination. For babies, who are so utterly helpless and dependent, no theory is as important as a theory of love. From the time they are very small babies are figuring out these theories of love, based on what they see the caregivers around them do and say. And these theories in turn shape the way these babies will care for their own children when they grow up.

Knowledge about love, like other kinds of knowledge, leads babies to imagine how their caregivers will act and how they should act themselves. These predictions and actions lead to the vicious and benign cycles that are so characteristically human. But imagination also gives babies, and the rest of us, a way to escape those cycles. Even a little evidence lets children imagine other, better ways that love might work.

"But what about immortality?" ten-year-old Alison asks. I suspect that she, like Woody Allen, would have said that she didn't want to achieve immortality through her children, she wanted to achieve it through not dying. Failing that, though, children aren't bad. One of the worst things about writing about the importance of children is that practically everything you say turns out to sound like a greeting card. Still, clichés often get to be clichés because they're true, and the cliché that children are our future is no more than simple, literal truth.

For human children the cliché runs particularly deep. Children are not just our future because they carry on our genes. For human beings, in particular, our sense of who we are, both as individuals and as a group, is intimately tied to where we come from and where we're going, to our past and our future. The human capacity for change means that we can't figure out what it is to be human just by looking at the way we are now. We need instead to peer forward into the vast ramifying space of human possibilities. The explorers we see out there at the farthest edge look very much like our children.

Notes

*

Science and philosophy rest on the achievements of thousands of precursors, and for a book as wide-ranging as this one, a really complete list of references would go on for hundreds of pages. Since most readers of this book will not be professional philosophers or scientists, I've used a different approach. In the notes, I've directed the reader to at least one source for each empirical fact I've talked about in the book. I've also tried to refer to review articles that will give the reader a big picture of lots of experiments and data. And I've tried to flag books that I think are particularly significant or helpful.

INTRODUCTION

6   Encyclopedia of Philosophy: Edwards 1967; Craig 1998.
7   *"evolutionary psychology"*: Pinker 1997; Barkow et al. 1994.
11 *Babies' brains seem to have*: For some reviews of brain development findings see Huttenlocher 2002a, b; Johnson et al. 2002; Dawson and Fischer 1994.
12 *They involve the prefrontal cortex*: For a review of prefrontal cortex development see Krasnegor et al. 1997.
13 *"inhibition"*: Diamond 2002.
13 *plastic frontal lobes*: Shaw et al. 2006.

1: POSSIBLE WORLDS

19   *"counterfactuals"*: Lewis 1986.
22   *Who is more upset?*: Tversky and Kahneman 1973.
22   *bronze medalist or the silver?*: Medvec et al. 1995.
24   *standard baby toy*: This ring task, and the rake task that follows, were adapted from Uzgiris and Hunt 1975. See Gopnik 1982; Gopnik and Meltzoff 1986.
25   *right kinds of information*: Willatts 1999.
25   *little evidence that chimpanzees*: Povinelli et al. 2000.
25   *smart birds like crows*: Bluff et al. 2007.
25   *success of* Homo sapiens: Byrne 2002.
26   *psychologist Paul Harris*: Harris's book (Harris 2000) is by far the best review and discussion of children's pretense and imagination.
26   *English countryside story*: Harris et al. 1996.
26   *if you put them in order*: Sobel 2002, 2004.
27   *eighteen months old or even younger*: Belsky and Most 1981; Lillard 2002; Leslie 1987.
29   *use tools in an insightful way*: Gopnik 1982; Gopnik and Meltzoff 1986.
29   *you'll need a broom*: Harris 2000.
30   *"just pretend"*: Lillard and Witherington 2004.
30   *not the pretend one*: Woolley and Wellman 1990, 1993.
31   *cat just by thinking about it*: Wellman and Estes 1986.
31   *gingerly moved away from the box*: Harris 2000.
31   *they still wouldn't drink it*: Rozin et al. 1990.
32   *causal knowledge and counterfactual thinking*: Lewis 1986.
33   *make that future real*: The idea that causality can be understood in terms of interventions has been articulated most persuasively and extensively by James Woodward in Woodward 2003.
35   *Piaget*: Piaget 1954.
36   *good logical explanations all the same*: Hickling and Wellman 2001.
36   *invisible germs make you ill*: Gelman 2003.
36   *their understanding of life and death*: Inagaki and Hatano 2006.
38   *knowledge to discriminate possibilities*: Schult and Wellman 1997.
39   *"cognitive maps"*: Tolman 1948; O'Keefe and Nadel 1979.
41   *complex causal relations among events*: Gopnik et al. 2004.
41   *draw all these consequences*: Inagaki and Hatano 2006; Gelman 2003.
42   *give a mathematical account*: Spirtes et al. 1993.
42   *that scientific experts make*: Pearl 2000.
44   *counterfactual predictions*: Gopnik et al. 2001.
45   *same experiment in a different way*: Schulz and Gopnik 2004.

2: IMAGINARY COMPANIONS

48   *"Machiavellian intelligence"*: Byrne and Whiten 1988.
49   *psychologist Marjorie Taylor*: Marjorie Taylor's wonderful book (Taylor 1999) is the source for much of this chapter.

51 *imaginary friend was Charlie Ravioli*: Gopnik 2002.

55 *theory of the mind*: This has become an enormous area of research. For good reviews see Astington 1993; Flavell 1999; and Wellman 2002.

55 *broccoli and Goldfish crackers*: Repacholi and Gopnik 1997.

56 *raw broccoli or Cheerios*: Wellman et al. 2000.

56 *there are pencils in there!*: Wimmer and Perner 1983. For a meta-analysis see Wellman et al. 2001. Some recent work may show that even younger children can do this.

56 *children's everyday explanations*: Bartsch and Wellman 1995.

58 *they are also better liars*: LaLonde and Chandler 1995.

58 *the same thing in experiments*: Sodian et al. 1991; Talwar and Lee 2002.

59 *"executive control"*: Carlson and Moses 2001; Carlson et al. 2004.

59 *"delay of gratification" experiments*: Mischel et al. 1989.

62 *people with autism*: Grandin 1995; Gopnik et al. 2005.

62 the Dog in the Night-Time: Haddon 2004.

62 *theory of other people's minds*: Baron-Cohen 1995; Baron-Cohen et al. 2005.

63 *what pretend play is all about*: Baron-Cohen et al. 2005.

63 *Henry James*: James 1909.

69 *engineers of human souls*: Škvorecký 1999.

70 Lord of the Rings: Auden 1956.

72 *changes in inhibition*: e.g., Diamond 2002.

3: ESCAPING PLATO'S CAVE

75 *Plato's* Republic: Plato translated by Jowett 1888.

76 *learning techniques that scientists use*: Carey 1985; Gopnik 1988; Wellman and Gelman 1992.

76 *David Hume*: Hume 2007. Originally published 1748.

77 *actually learn about the world*: Spirtes et al. 1993; Glymour et al. 1988; Scheines et al. 1998.

78 *Reverend Thomas Bayes*: Bayes 1963; Griffiths et al. 2008. Also see Wikipedia on Bayes for a good brief explanation of Bayesianism.

79 *The famous Turing test*: Turing 1950.

80 *rocks on Mars*: Ramsey et al. 2002.

80 *turns a genome into an organism*: e.g., Helman et al. 2004 (there are many more).

80 *causes monsoons in India*: Steinbach et al. 2003.

81 *sensitive to statistical patterns*: Saffran et al. 1996.

83 *the beginning of music appreciation*: Saffran et al. 1999.

83 *often see a window nearby*: Kirkham et al. 2002; Aslin et al. 1998.

83 *some important statistical ideas*: Xu and Garcia 2008.

83 *two and a half, and probably earlier*: Sobel and Kirkham 2006.

83 *make genuinely causal inferences*: Gopnik et al. 2001; Sobel et al. 2004.

85 *the detector than the first one*: Kushnir and Gopnik 2005.

85 *probability of causes and effects*: Sobel et al. 2004.

87 *results than observation alone*: Eberhardt and Scheines 2007.

87   *happy because the experiment succeeds*: Papousek et al. 1987.
88   *to make the mobile move*: For a review of many of these mobile studies see Rovee-Collier and Barr 2001.
88   *Piaget described this kind*: Piaget 1952a, b.
88   *the gear toy*: Schulz et al. 2007.
90   *to figure out causal problems*: Schulz and Bonawitz 2007.
90   *Christine Legare*: Legare et al. 2008.
93   *directed toward particular goals*: Woodward 1998.
94   *and actions of other people*: Meltzoff and Moore 1977, 1983.
94   *results of those actions*: Meltzoff 1988.
94   *using your head instead*: Gergely et al. 2002.
94   *dumbbell, as Meltzoff did*: Meltzoff 1995.
95   *perform the experiments themselves*: Schulz et al. 2007.
95   *Barbara Rogoff studied Mayan*: Rogoff 1990.
98   *to differentiate people and things*: Watson 1972.
98   *psychologist Susan Johnson*: Johnson et al. 2007a, b, 2008; Shimizu and Johnson 2004.
98   *the blicket detector*: Schulz and Gopnik 2004.
100 *act similarly in those situations*: Zimbardo 2007.
100 *to test what was wrong*: Weinberg and Tronick 1996; Gusella et al. 1988.
100 *mimicking everything that the baby did*: Meltzoff 2007.
101 *IQ and verbal tests*: Ruffman et al. 1998; Sulloway 1996.
101 *the minds of others*: For a review and meta-analysis see Milligan et al. 2007.
102 *until they are eight or nine*: Peterson and Siegal 1995.
102 *Jennie Pyers*: Pyers 2005.

4: WHAT IS IT LIKE TO BE A BABY?

107 *Thomas Nagel*: Nagel 1974.
108 *"blindsight"*: Christensen et al. 2008; Weizkrantz 2007.
109 *smooth, unbroken visual field*: Dennett 1992.
110 *Peter Singer*: Singer 1976.
111 *endogenous attention*: Posner 2004.
111 *associated with attention*: e.g., Polich 2003; Knight and Scabini 1998.
112 *"inattentional blindness"*: Mack and Rock 1998; Simons and Chabris 1999.
113 *particular kind of chemical*: For a review of the role of neurotransmitters in attention see Robbins et al. 2004.
114 *Merzenich and his colleagues*: e.g., Polley et al. 2006; Recanzone et al. 1992a, b.
114 *cholinergic transmitters*: e.g., Metherate and Weinberger 1989; Blake et al. 2002.
116 *their capacity for attention*: For reviews on infant attention see Ruff and Rothbart 1996; Colombo 2004; Richards 2004. John Colombo provided very helpful information for this discussion.
118 *give children a memory task*: Hagen and Hale 1972.

120 *anesthetics act on these neurotransmitters*: Taylor and Lerman 1991; Lerman et al. 1983.

120 *young animals' cells changed*: Zhang et al. 2001; de Villers-Sidani et al. 2007.

120 *quite early in infancy*: Colombo 2004.

121 *Rafael Malach*: Goldberg et al. 2006; Golland et al. 2007.

122 *prune more connections*: Huttenlocher 2002a, b; Johnson et al. 2002.

124 *philosophically intriguing results*: Flavell et al. 1995a, b, 1997, 1999, 2000.

129 *"flow"*: Csíkszentmihályi 1992.

130 *"beginner's mind"*: Suzuki and Brown 2002.

130 *meteoric showers of images*: James 2001.

5: WHO AM I?

134 *sea slugs have that kind*: Rankin et al. 1987.

135 *episodic or autobiographical memory*: For a review see Tulving 2002.

135 *his initials as H.M.*: Scoville and Milner 1957; Corkin 2002.

136 Challenger *disaster shortly after*: Neisser and Harsch 1992.

136 *creating false memories*: Loftus 1997a, b.

137 *abducted by aliens*: Clancy 2005.

138 *occurred to them in the past*: Fivush et al. 1987.

138 *into a continuous narrative*: Nelson and Fivush 2004.

140 *free recall*: Ornstein et al. 2006.

141 *trouble with sources*: Shimamura and Squire 1987.

141 *where their beliefs come from*: Gopnik and Graf 1988; O'Neill and Gopnik 1991.

142 *their understanding of sources*: Giles et al. 2002.

143 *"false belief" experiment*: Gopnik and Astington 1988; Gopnik and Slaughter 1991.

145 *philosopher John Campbell*: Campbell 1994.

145 *recognize themselves in the mirror*: Brooks-Gunn and Lewis 1984.

145 *Teresa McCormack*: McCormack and Hoerl 2005, 2007.

146 *more dramatic experiment*: Povinelli et al. 1999.

147 *Cristina Atance*: Atance and Meltzoff 2005; Atance and O'Neill 2005.

149 *philosopher Jerry Fodor*: Fodor 1998.

150 *what the Flavells did*: Flavell et al. 1997.

159 *couldn't tolerate the delay*: Mischel et al. 1989.

159 *aboriginal communities in Canada*: Chandler and Proulx 2006.

161 *irrational unconscious bias*: Wegner 2002.

161 *notably Daniel Dennett*: Dennett and Weiner 1991.

161 *Paul and Patricia Churchland*: Churchland 1995, 2002.

161 *John Searle and David Chalmers*: Searle 1992; Chalmers 1996.

163 *experience those changes themselves*: For a more extended philosophical discussion of this point see Gopnik 1993.

6: HERACLITUS' RIVER AND THE ROMANIAN ORPHANS

165 *What should she do?*: Parfit 1984, p. 145.

168 *Romanian orphanages*: The most extensive, exhaustive, and masterful work on the fate of the Romanian orphans has been done by Michael Rutter and his colleagues. See, e.g., Rutter et al. 2004, 2007; Beckett et al. 2006. Also see Rutter 2006 for an excellent review of the interplay of genes and environments.

170 *"heritability"*: For heritability and twin and adoption studies see Plomin 1994.

171 *alcoholism is heritable*: Dick and Beirut 2006.

172 *Eric Turkheimer*: Turkheimer et al. 2003.

172 The Bell Curve: Herrnstein and Murray 1994.

173 *although our genes have remained the same*: This is known as the "Flynn effect." See Flynn 1987; Dickens and Flynn 2001.

174 *experience stressful events*: Kendler and Prescott 2006.

175 *cases of abuse*: For a recent review see Cicchetti and Valentino 2006.

175 *list of other ills*: For good reviews of this literature see Rutter 2006; Kendler and Prescott 2006.

177 *poor children's early experiences*: For a readable recent review of the effects of early preschool interventions see Kirp 2007.

7: LEARNING TO LOVE

180 *leave them and then return*: The classic reference is Ainsworth et al. 1978. There have been hundreds of other studies since.

180 *mother's face and voice*: DeCasper and Fifer 1980; Field et al. 1984.

181 *the statistics of love*: Ainsworth 1993.

181 *Romanian orphans*: Rutter et al. 2004, 2007.

181 *not all babies learn the same things*: Ainsworth et al. 1978.

182 *inside the babies are miserable*: Spangler and Grossman 1993.

182 *cultural differences*: Van Ijzendoorn and Kroonenberg 1988.

183 *"Disorganized" babies*: Main and Solomon 1986.

183 *"internal working models"*: Bowlby 1980; Main et al. 1985.

183 *based on the evidence*: Ainsworth 1993; Blehar et al. 1977.

184 *different theories of love*: Johnson et al. 2007a.

184 *at five or six*: Main et al. 1985.

185 *poet Robert Hass*: From "Dragonflies Mating," Hass 1996.

186 *theories in many ways*: For a recent review of adult attachment see Mikulincer and Shaver 2007.

186 *loved ones at the airport*: Fraley and Shaver 1998.

187 *Serena Chen*: Chen et al. 1999; Chen 2003.

188 *expecting their first baby*: Benoit and Parker 1994.

189 *thirty or forty years*: For a good review of these studies see Grossman et al. 2005.

192 *social monogamy*: See, e.g., Reichard and Boesche 2003.